DON'T LEAVE ME

THIS WAY

DON'T LEAVE ME THIS WAY

or when i get back on my
feet you'll be sorry

julia fox garrison

HarperCollins*Publishers*

Names and identifying details of some individuals have been changed to
protect their privacy, and sequences of some events have been altered and
times compressed for narrative flow. Except for these minor changes, the
events in this book happened just as they are described.

HarperCollins books may be purchased for educational, business, or sales
promotional use. For information, please write: Special Markets Department, HarperCollins Publishers, 10 East 53rd Street, New York, NY
10022.

FIRST HARPERCOLLINS EDITION

Designed by Renata Di Biase

Printed on acid-free paper

Library of Congress Cataloging-in-Publication Data

Garrison, Julia Fox.
    Don't leave me this way: or when I get back on my feet you'll be sorry /
Julia Fox Garrison.—1st ed.
        p.   cm.
    ISBN-10: 0-06-112061-8
    ISBN-13: 978-0-06-112061-9
        1. Garrison, Julia Fox—Health. 2. Cerebrovascular disease—Patients—
Biography. 3. Cerebrovascular disease—Patients—Rehabilitation. I. Title.

RC388.5.G42 2006
362.196'810092—dc22
[B]
                                                                2005055032

06 07 08 09 10 ❖/RRD 10 9 8 7 6 5 4 3 2 1

To Jim, for your unwavering support. You are my rock; I am honored to be your "hard place."

To Rory, for understanding and accepting that I could still be a mother. You are my inspiration.

Because of you both, I continue to strive and thrive.

DON'T LEAVE ME

THIS WAY

partONE

One of the Rats
in the Race

⊞

SHE WAS SOUTHBOUND ON ROUTE 128, driving to work and doing her daily ritual, thanking God for her son, Rory, and her husband, Jim, and all of her family and her friends and her job and the fact that she and Jim were talking about having another baby and the fact that she had lost weight thanks to that stuff she was taking and the fact that she had a good marriage, and she finished thanking God and quickly glanced in the rearview mirror and changed lanes confidently and safely and started thinking about precisely how she was going to handle the switchover of the phone system at work while making everything look SEAMLESS to the customers calling in, customers who didn't know (and didn't much care) that her company was moving from one building to another, or that BIG, BIG CHANGES were in the works. And she thought, *Bring it on.*

Southbound on 128. And she thought, *Seamless.*

And as she was driving it didn't occur to her to thank God for the ability to stand, or to walk, or to drive, or to take a shower herself, or to dress herself, or to have a functioning circulatory system, or to make her way to the toilet unescorted, or to change her own tampon rather than watch helplessly as a total stranger did so, or to wipe her own ass for that matter. And *had* she thought of these things she would certainly have been thankful to God for them, but as of the morning of July 17, 1997, it had never occurred to her to even notice them, much less express gratitude for them.

Southbound on 128 and driving and thinking that last week her boss had sat her down and told her "Big, big changes are in the works," and "I'll be honest with you, the company is going through a major transition," and "We need you to keep everybody in your department upbeat, that's what you're so good at," and "Don't get me wrong, this is a question of survival," and "You're the best team player we've got," and "The transition has to be seamless." Big, big changes in the works. "Don't let them throw you."

Southbound on 128 and remembering the huge cutout of Babe Ruth she'd put together for the party with the president when he introduced his new management team and the theme was "The Winning Team." She'd managed to track down a life-size stand-up photo of the Babe and she'd put a baseball cap with the company logo on it and it got a standing ovation. She'd decorated her department with a baseball theme, even hiring a hot dog and popcorn vendor. There were different positions for her coworkers to play— the batting cage, the pitching mound. Boosting morale within the company. Big, big changes were in the works and everything was going to be seamless, goddammit, *seamless*.

Southbound on 128, a little sleepy, time to wake up now, thankful that she knew the road as well as she did. Thankful she knew exactly what was in front of her. *Bring it on.*

A long time ago you had a vision.

"You're going to be in a wheelchair for a while. But it's going to make you a better person."

You saw yourself in a wheelchair in the dream. When you woke up you felt confused.

■ ■ ■

HER NORMAL ROUTINE WAS THAT SHE WOULD take a lunchtime walk with Berkeley, the other customer support manager; together, they would walk close to four miles in under an hour, and discuss department strategies while they got in a little exercise. On July 17, they both had to go to separate manager events, so they decided not to walk at lunchtime. She was feeling congested and tired and was slightly relieved that they were not going to be walking.

She sent out a short e-mail to her department, asking if anyone had some kind of cold medicine. She wanted to use it to help relieve her symptoms so she could continue with her plans for the day.

A coworker responded: "I picked up some over-the-counter stuff at the pharmacy; you're welcome to it."

She swung by the cubicle, picked up the medicine, headed to the bathroom, swigged some water, and got on with her day.

AT NOON SHE WENT TO THE BUILDING cafeteria and made a salad from the salad bar.

She had the salad in her office while she composed an e-mail regarding her department's imminent move to another facility, which was scheduled for the end of the week. She was planning on staying at the local hotel over the weekend to oversee the relocation. A coworker came by her office to ask if she wanted a ride to the manager's event in Tyngsboro. She said she was still writing the e-mail with the details of everyone's responsibilities for the move. "Go on ahead and I'll meet you there," she said.

At a little past two, she felt a throbbing pain in the right side of her head.

It was as if a switch had been flipped. The pain was immediate—a volcano erupting inside her skull.

SHE SAW RANDY, THE DEPARTMENT VICE PRESIDENT, and told him she had a throbbing headache. He suggested going to the bathroom and trying to throw up. He seemed to think that the pressure would release if she threw up her breakfast. The idea didn't exactly bathe her in relief.

The pain was now excruciating.

She knew it was serious. She knew she had to go to the hospital. She was unsure what hospital she should go to. There was the hospital where she had delivered her son, but it was not a hospital her primary care provider was affiliated with. Her new primary care doctor was about thirty-five miles away. The sister hospital was about ten miles away. She had to make a choice. But her head wasn't working in its usual optimal choice-making mode. She needed some help.

She asked Caryn, the department administrative assistant, to call her doctor and tell her she was experiencing severe head pain and that it was urgent. The doctor's office put Caryn on hold for a few minutes.

Time started to shudder.

She heard Caryn shouting into the telephone.

She looked for a position that would alleviate the pain. She tried sitting, pacing, then lying on the floor. Nothing stopped the shooting pain.

She knew Berkeley would be leaving soon to attend the meeting that was being held in Boston, so asking him to drive to the hospital was out. She asked Caryn to drive her to the hospital. Time shuddered again, compressed and expanded.

She passed Berkeley in the corridor and realized she must look odd, because he was suddenly very concerned when he saw her. His face seemed to contort, mirroring hers. He asked if she was all right. Time compressed suddenly, then expanded again, and she was in Caryn's car.

Caryn was hurtling northbound on 128. The pain was like a volcano. She thought about screaming at her to go faster. But for some reason she heard her own voice saying, in a matter-of-fact tone:

"I'm dying."

You Want a Smoke?

CARYN'S CAR evaporates.

She's in the hospital parking lot and for some lunatic reason she announces that it's going to be too expensive to go into the emergency room. With her head steadily intensifying to Chernobyl status, she makes Caryn take her all the way up to the fourth floor, where the walk-in room for outpatients is located. Space is rippling visibly before her in the waiting room. When people talk, their words get heavy and thud to the floor before reaching her. The nurse says something to her but not enough words make it through the wall. The nurse seems Slow. Deliberate. Intense. And there's no logic, at least none that she can make out.

Caryn translates. It turns out she's supposed to go to the emergency room after all.

Time shudders again and the triage nurse is taking her blood pressure and it's a little low but (according to Caryn, translating the nurse) "not an alarming range." And she does feel calm for some reason, even with waves of pain that make the room flash and disappear. She realizes she's in the emergency room's corridor. An elderly man and woman, bleeding, are wheeled past her on two gurneys. She hears the words "auto accident." The room goes white with pain again.

Now *she's* on a gurney, a narrow corridor that smells of alcohol is consuming her, and Caryn is receding into the edges of her peripheral vision. She shouts out, "Call Jim. He's my husband. Have him paged and tell him to get my entire family over here because I'm not going to make it." Caryn knows Jim is her husband but for some reason she wants to make this point absolutely clear to her.

The corridor throws Caryn away and she listens to the wheels rattle and stares at the ceiling as it hurtles past above her. Time shudders and then Caryn is back again next to her and she's still staring at the ceiling but she's not moving anymore. The only thing that's moving is the wave of white pain in her skull.

She says, "Caryn, hold my hand." She does and she squeezes her hand hard because the pain is right on top of her skull and she thinks she is going to die then and there. She doesn't know it at the time, but every time her heart beats, every time her pulse throbs, it releases blood into her brain. On the count of two. Every time she counts to two, she hits a wave of pain. It bursts and explodes. She can't catch her breath.

Time quivers and the room goes bright with the pain and when it lightens up again she is throwing up, just like Randy had suggested back at work, only it doesn't seem to be helping much. As she vomits, people are taking off her jewelry and shouting and she hears scissors cutting her blouse and bra away and a tube goes down her throat and the gurney is moving again and Jim flashes by and they lead him away and she feels bad that he has to see her this way and the tube in her throat comes out again and a male nurse is running next to her as she plunges down the corridor on her gurney and he's telling her to grab his fingers hard.

She tries, but she can't see his fingers.

They're a blur, moving slowly in the air. It's like some trippy sixties film, moving frame by frame. She can't manage to get a fix on them. She orders her hand to reach out to where his fingers ought to be, but her hand refuses to respond.

Is he doing magic tricks with his hands to make his fingers fade in and out?

She's having a stroke.

Instantly she feels a calm place in the middle of the pain and she says to the guy pushing her down the hallway, "Am I having a stroke?" And the ceiling is getting lighter and lighter because another wave of pain is coming.

He doesn't look at her, though, he keeps staring straight ahead, but he smiles on purpose and says, "What did you say? You want a smoke?"

She realizes he's making a joke for her and she thinks it would probably be polite if she laughed, but then the ceiling vanishes, white.

She is gone.

Karen Croaked, Too

Don't worry.
Life will go on.
You're a fighter.
You have purpose.
You have a mission.

SOMEONE IS TELLING you to wake up.

You open your eyes, feeling empty in a white room that won't tell you anything about how it met you. Your head is throbbing and you are staring at the ceiling and your peripheral vision says you are surrounded by your family and you can hear some of them saying you should wake up and they sound dangerously, oddly happy, purposefully happy for your benefit, and it is obvious to you now that Something Has Happened.

You try to turn over to look at your family. But the left side of your body refuses to obey any command from you.

It's not really you. Your left side lies frozen. You wonder, *Why are they using straps on me?*

You try to turn again. No doubt about it now. Not only will

your body not obey you—it is also totally numb on the left side. It doesn't exist.

This is what you found out later: Your mom had been saying the rosary while you were having emergency brain surgery. Your other family members had been mostly pacing. One of the neuro-surgeons from the operating team appeared in the room where your family was sequestered. "Who are all these people?" he asked, stepping into the room where sixteen people waited. "We're her family," your brother Jeff replied.

"She is in critical condition. She appears to have had a seizure and she had heart failure. Her hemorrhage is massive. We're doing life-saving measures to evacuate the blood. If she makes it, she'll most likely need further reparative surgery once she's been stabilized."

"What do you mean 'if she makes it'? She's healthy, young, and strong," Jim said incredulously.

"What I'm saying is that she may not survive the operation. This procedure has a high mortality rate," the surgeon said solemnly. He turned and left as abruptly as he'd entered.

Silence.

As if to break the tension, your brother Joe blurted out, "Let's all send her some positive energy." To which your father instantly responded, "Shut the hell up, Joe."

YOU HAVE TUBES COMING OUT of everywhere. You move your hand to your face to feel where the tubes go, but time shudders and you're gone again.

You will definitely be someplace after this part.
You will occupy space again and time will pass for you again.
When you get there you will see people who love you.

SOMEONE IS TELLING you to wake up.

"How did she know she was having a stroke? Is she in a risk group?"

"No, not from what's here."

"Are you sure that's what she said? 'Am I having a stroke?'"

"He's got it on the report."

"Is she waking up?"

Silence.

"Are you waking up, Julia?"

WAIT A MINUTE MAYBE that was about the other time there *was* another time when people who love you *were* saying wake up Julia wake up there *was* a time when . . .

"Hi. We're going to be your radiology team. I'm Doctor Doogie and this is Doctor Radio. We think you may have an AVM."

"Arterial vascular malformation."

"That's an inherent weakness in the blood vessels."

"It's usually congenital."

"You're going to have an angiogram."

Two doctors. Two assistants. They wheel you into the white, brightly lit, sterile room for an angiogram. Whatever that is. There's music playing in the background, James Taylor's "Fire and Rain."

"Not a great song, guys," you mutter.

"Why's that?" says Dr. Doogie.

"Why's that? Suzanne doesn't make it! That's why's that."

The nurse assistant smiles and leans in so she's next to your face and asks if you'd rather hear a Carpenters CD.

This gives you pause.

It occurs to you that Karen Carpenter croaked, too.

"Don't bother."

They hoist your (foreign) body onto a narrow slab and give you painkillers and strip you naked and shave off your pubic hair and swab you with antiseptics and put a white disk about two inches from your nose. You say, "Before you get started, let's get one thing straight. I don't want to hear any 'oops' shit from you guys."

Nobody laughs.

James Taylor sings on: "Suzanne, the plans they made put an end to you . . ."

"Lie *completely* still and stay alert. No movement whatsoever."

"Hey," you say, "on the left side, that's going to be no problem, but my right side may misbehave . . ."

No laughter. They tell you at least five times that you have to be awake and stay completely still. Any mistake could cause internal bleeding and possibly death.

You think, *This is a pretty serious group of people I'm dealing with.*

They talk among themselves about how tall you are and how long a rod they're going to need: Dr. Radio says, "Get the eight-footer."

"Hey," you call out, "I'm only five foot six! Where's the extra going to go, through the hole in my head?"

Little pause, then they continue discussing among themselves.

Then they cut a hole in your groin area and start inserting a long, flexible steel rod through the hole into an artery. They snake the rod all the way through, up to your brain. They can see where the rod goes on a display screen in front of them.

They bounce the rod off your femur to make sure the placement is correct. It hurts like hell. You groan.

The assistant asks, "Are you comfortable?"

"Well," you say, "I'd be *more* comfortable in a Barcalounger."

"Better pump up the painkillers."

They snake the rod all the way up to your brain and talk in little whispers about what they see.

"Hey," you say, "how's the fishing? Catch anything yet?"

Then they snake it back out again and the nurse applies pressure to the entry site. She tells you it's a deep puncture wound and she puts heavy pressure on your groin for at least five minutes so the blood can clot.

You make a mental note to remind your family members not to get an angiogram if they can possibly avoid it.

After all that effort to stay awake, you can't really sleep when they send you back to the intensive care unit (ICU). Which is actually fortunate since you have to be completely still for eight hours. They sandbag your right leg to prevent movement.

Eventually they unsandbag you and you sleep a deep, black sleep. You have a weird dream about how to become a better person by letting someone staple your head.

When you wake up you need to remain completely still and perpendicular for eight hours. It's quite a feat drinking from a straw without lifting your head.

After the surgery, you feel as though you'll explode from the pressure to urinate. After having a rod in your groin, you can't go on your own. Put a fountainhead on your stomach and you'd rival any Disney display.

Half a Clock

Your mother tells you that Edie is having a hard time. Edie was in a bridge club with your mother for thirty years, and your mother mentions that Edie is having a hard time. You think to yourself, I should really stop in and see Edie.

MORNING SNAPS INTO PLACE and someone tells you to wake up and the doctors are gathered in front of your bed and they congratulate you. You were very perceptive: You have in fact had a stroke. Then they tell you the angio shows no evidence of an AVM. They feel "perplexed" as to what your condition might be.

One of the doctors—your dad says later that he's very famous—tells you that you should think of your brain's large and small blood vessels as having berries on them. Then he says he has no idea what that means, since an AVM is no longer a possibility. He promises the team will keep you posted when they know what's going to happen next.

"Unless my brain beats you to it!" you warn them.

Somber faces on Jim, your brother John, and your dad. Here is one of the leading radiologists in the country shrugging, saying he doesn't know what you have. Everyone's quiet. Lots of questions. No answers.

You stare at the doctors. They leave. One of the nurses stays behind.

You tell your husband you're a little disappointed that you don't have an AVM, because you wanted a definite diagnosis and you could use some hard information. You must be starting to cry because the nurse wipes the left side of your face. The nurse says you should be relieved that you didn't have an AVM, since treatment is difficult and can be fatal.

You're going to be a better person.

SO. YOU DON'T HAVE AN AVM. What *do* you have? Whatever it is, it apparently involves having berries on the brain. *Unless you're in a strawberry patch,* you think to yourself, *berries on the brain does not sound like what you want.*

The next morning another doctor describes your brain vessels as "sausagelike."

"If we're not talking about the morning menu," you say, "sausage doesn't sound good."

You begin to wonder whether the doctors are hungry and looking forward to breakfast. Next, they'll be cracking an egg in a basin and saying, "This is your brain, and this is your brain hemorrhaging," as they scramble the contents.

YOU HAVE BEEN IN INTENSIVE CARE for approximately a week. People come and go and you keep getting medication and time shudders and shimmers and twists as it sees fit.

Morning snaps into place and your family is now visiting you. Flies are swarming around your mom and dad. You keep swatting them with your right hand, the only hand that will move for you. You keep saying, "Don't you see them? They're all over Dad's head." Waving that right hand, trying to swat the flies.

"No flies on me . . . but they are sure loving Mom and Dad, aren't they?"

Silence. Quizzical faces.

"You don't see them, do you?"

Your parents shake their heads.

Your mind is capable of manufacturing flies. But it cannot manufacture sensation on the left side of your body.

Morning wobbles and collapses and it's dark outside and Jim is watching as they change your bandages. You don't know what you look like because no one will give you a mirror, not even Jim. Dr. Neuro has told Jim not to give you a mirror.

It occurs to you that this is not good.

You try to catch a glimpse of yourself in the window across the room.

It's only a second, the picture you see in the dark night window, but it makes your heart feel hollow and cold. The right side of your head is void of any hair and there is a huge S-shaped incision starting at the top of your scalp and extending below your right ear. The incision is stamped shut with staples.

Was that another illusion your mind conjured up? Or was that really you?

You look away and ask the nurse to pull the curtain on the window so the reflection doesn't show. She starts to do this but twists into nothingness before her hand touches the curtain.

"TAKE THIS PEN. Draw a clock showing the time ten–fifty. Ten five oh. Draw the clock right here on this sheet."

One of the neurology residents. Apparently you're in the middle of some kind of test. Bright daylight again.

Jim says, "Come on, honey. You know how to do this."

"What time am I drawing on the clock?"

"Ten–fifty. Ten five oh."

You take the pen and draw this:

Jim frowns and urges you to do it again. The neurology guy takes notes. You don't want to disappoint Jim. You ask to try again. The neurology guy says, "Okay."

It comes out the same.

"Now draw a clock with all the numbers, one to twelve."

You draw this:

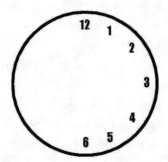

Half a clock. It looks utterly wrong. But you can't think what will fix it.

Nothing exists on the left side of your world. You glance up at Jim. His face is completely crestfallen. You can sense he's beginning to get an idea of the magnitude of your injury. It's not just the left side of your body. It's your brain. It's your command center.

The neurology guy sniffs and nods and writes something down.

"Okay, let's try something different. Count backward by sevens from one hundred."

You take a deep breath.

"Okay. One hundred . . ."

Silence.

"Go ahead." He is so damn smug.

"One hundred . . ."

"Yes."

"Nothing's coming."

The neurology guy smirks and sniffs again and takes more notes.

"Don't write that down."

It's Jim. He's mad.

"Why not?" the neurology guy asks.

"Because she couldn't have counted backward from one hundred by sevens *before* the stroke."

The resident stares at Jim, then looks down at his clipboard and keeps writing.

You shout out: *"Stop writing!"*

He stops and stares at you.

"How the hell do *you* know," you demand, "that I wasn't stupid before my stroke?"

"You are suffering," the resident says flatly, "from left-side neglect. It's a common symptom of a right-hemisphere stroke. It may or may not go away."

"Does that mean," you ask, "that if I don't like listening to you, I can have you stand on my left side, and you'll go away?"

He stares at you both like you have just escaped from a lunatic asylum. But he stops writing. He puts the clipboard on the wall and leaves.

Your Encounter with
the Tapioca Lady

A ladder and a choice.
Going to be there climbing it.
But going to have to choose, too.

"I RECOMMEND chemotherapy."

Nighttime again. For some reason there's a doctor standing by the bed. He seems to think you know him—short, bald, red-faced, and fat, in a white coat. A baby who has been poorly extended into the dimensions of the adult world.

So it's you and the bed and the white sheet drawn across you and the window with the curtain drawn to block the night and the smell of antiseptic and Jim standing next to you, always Jim standing next to you, thank God, and then this impossible doctor-infant, pudgy and crimson-faced, clutching a ballpoint pen in broad fingers wrapped into a tight, shut fist.

"I'm definitely recommending chemotherapy. Actually it's not a recommendation. It's your only option. There are sterility issues, but that shouldn't be your concern anymore."

He seems to want one of you to say something. Jim stares him down.

"People sometimes get emotional about the sterility issue. Don't do that. You've got a good family already, yes? Anyway, first an echocardiogram, to confirm there was no damage to the heart, and make sure that wasn't what caused your stroke. Then chemotherapy."

He is paid, apparently, to radiate a single red idea: *I've made up my mind about this because I know more than you do.*

Dr. Jerk.

"You have vasculitis. I've never seen it affect the brain before, but that's definitely what it is. Normally affects the lower large organs. It's incurable. Can go into remission, though, if you're lucky. Not much luck so far, of course, in your case, but there you go. At any rate, the treatment is chemotherapy and high doses of prednisone. The physical problems, I'm afraid, are permanent. Bad news is, you're going to have to get used to doing things very differently. Good news is, at least you'll have better parking possibilities."

Silence.

"What with the handicapped sticker, I mean."

Jim glares at him.

"What," you ask, "is an echocardiogram?"

THEY ARE WHEELING YOU on a gurney through the halls. The metal railing of the gurney sends little shock waves down your whole left side, like the sensation you get when you bite down on tinfoil with a filling.

"Why couldn't they pad the railings?"

The nurse is a huge linebacker type with a crew cut. He laughs—he thinks you're kidding—and asks if you're okay as he wheels you.

"What, exactly," you ask him, "is a drug-induced echocardiogram?"

He tells you.

■ ■ ■

JIM THERE, HOLDING YOUR HAND. You're together, in this tiny over-lit room. The tinier the room, the brighter they make it. You hold Jim's hand like you don't want to let go of it.

"Relax," Jim says. "It's not going to hurt."

You can't believe he said that.

"Jim, do you know what they're about to do to me?"

He puts his other hand on your hand and shakes his head no.

You tell him. It is basically an induced heart attack. They want to make your heart go crazy to see if they can make whatever happened to you happen again. They shoot you full of something and make your heart race like you just ran an Olympic track race. They're trying to confirm this vasculitis thing by coming within an inch of giving you a coronary and then stopping and bringing you back and monitoring what happened.

The linebacker crew cut nurse guy comes in and tells Jim he has to leave. He is arguing that he wants to stay but the bright room wobbles and twists and Jim is gone and there are now four nurses rammed into this closet of a room and you are being lifted onto a slab and the nurse says, "Don't let Dr. Jerk touch any of the equip-ment, he always screws it up."

You don't want to be here.

You don't want to have vasculitis. You don't want to have chemo-therapy.

You want to have another baby.

You say, out loud, "I want to have another baby."

The nurses stop what they're doing and look at you, then go back to setting up equipment and, evidently, dusting the tiny room for fingerprints.

The tiny room gets brighter and spins and Dr. Jerk is stand-ing over you and energetically messing with the equipment just like the nurses said he shouldn't. The nurses are trying to distract him by asking him about the monitors, but it's not working. He's really hyper; he's twisting every knob and pushing every button in sight.

You are a passenger on a tiny airplane and the Nutty Professor is in the cockpit.

You want to tell him that he isn't supposed to touch the equipment. You decide to say something, but the room bends again and your heart is racing inside your chest at a pace that could outdo any rock-and-roll drummer. Why on earth do you have to be awake for this?

"You should at least mist the patients," you say out loud. "Then they'd feel like they were having a good workout at the gym."

Nobody laughs.

Your heart continues its high-speed shudder. Dr. Jerk twists a dial and stares at the monitor.

A BIGGER SPACE SWIMS UP and snaps into place around you and it's morning and Jim kisses your forehead. "At least we've got a diagnosis."

You are in a different room, a different floor, but at least Jim's there to make it feel slightly less strange.

"Where is this?"

"The neurology floor. We've got a diagnosis, right?"

Dr. Jerk shimmers into existence on your left and Jim is gone and you're staring at the fat fingers clutching the pen again.

"I am still recommending chemotherapy. Sterility issues, of course. But there you go."

He's gone. You're alone. A nurse, tiny and wrinkled like a raisin, comes in and strips off the white sheet and turns you on your side. She is amazingly strong.

Although your left side is paralyzed, it is, you realize, hypersensitive to sensations—hot, cold, metals, and pain. You have a consistent pins-and-needles feeling on your left side from head to toe. A line could be drawn down the middle of your body, and everything on the left of that line—your left scalp, eyebrow, eye, nostril, gums, neck, shoulder, arm, hand, fingers, breast, stomach, thigh, knee, calf, ankle, foot, and toes—would not exist.

The raisin nurse pulls you into a sitting position by your shoulders. She is scary. It dawns on you that you cannot sit up by yourself. You have to be propped on several pillows like a doll placed on a bed—except you have a feeling you're not as cute.

You can't feed yourself, either. The raisin nurse spoons some oatmeal into your mouth.

TIME SLOWS to a crawl.

They keep coming into your room and drawing blood. Your mouth tastes like metal and your eyes won't stay shut. Every time they come to draw blood you ask for something that will help you sleep but they say as long as they're taking blood samples they can't give you anything and you are exhausted and you want to be able to dream your way out of this place.

Hours pass . . . you think. You don't understand time, but at any rate, absolutely nothing happens.

The doctor on call, a short dark-skinned man with salt-and-pepper hair and an accent, steps into your room and asks how you're doing. You can tell from his voice he's from another country, maybe India. You tell him you really need something to help you sleep and ask if he can do anything to help you. He looks at your chart and then leaves the room for what seems like eternity. You figure he must have seen on your chart that you are not supposed to have anything that would put you in a deep sleep. You think to yourself, *It's because they don't think I'll wake up.*

But he returns. He has a somber look on his face. He reaches for the light switch and turns it off.

This is his idea of helping you get to sleep. You can tell he feels bad and you half-expect him to lie down next to you and sing lullabies.

"Is there anything else I can do?" he asks.

"Could you help me count some sheep? I failed the counting test."

■ ■ ■

MORE TIME POURS out onto the floor, which brightens with a slim coating of dawn. A huge woman appears at the foot of your bed with a stack of five containers of tapioca pudding.

She barks in a gravelly voice: "Tapioca!"

You look at her quizzically.

"Huh?"

She seems somewhat annoyed and barks: "You ordered tapioca."

A memory—and a recent one, at that—flashes past. There was a speech pathologist. Blond hair. Serious eyes. She stared at your throat and spooned tapioca in your mouth to check your swallowing. The thick tapioca allowed her to track your swallowing mechanics.

This new tapioca woman must be here to do more tests.

You half-smile and say, "Are we going to do more tapioca testing?"

The tapioca woman's eyes scan your head, which, you suddenly remember, has a large incision with metal staples on the right side—and shoulder-length hair on the left.

You realize she probably thinks you just had a lobotomy.

She storms out of the room shaking her head, without leaving you any pudding.

The light in the room starts thickening and you feel something big and heavy drop over you and you wonder if you might be about to fall asleep, and you hear Jim saying, "No, don't wake her up, I'll just sit here with her."

You are climbing a ladder.
Actually it is more like a symbol of a ladder.
It's white and misty.
Something that uses the idea of a ladder to stand for something else.
Something bigger.
Anyway, you are climbing it.
You are moving upward.

The top of the ladder is hidden in white clouds.
You look around—
Sky
Ocean
Beautiful.
So simple.
Backdrop of blue sky.
Clouds above and below.
And you are on a ladder with no beginning and no end.
How close to God are you?
It's a grid going up, up, up.
You can keep climbing it if you want.
You have a choice.
You can keep climbing up and get closer to God,
Or you can go back to a body that doesn't work as well as it
     might.
You think,
"This isn't a dream. This is a choice."
You hear someone say,
"You're going to have to choose."
You choose to go back down and live your life better,
Become a better person,
But with the knowledge that it would have to be
In a different body.
You hear someone say,
"You pass over. You don't go away."

Shit Happens . . . but Only Occasionally

You are going to have to be strong for your family.

YOUR FAMILY ALWAYS LOOKS SO SAD when they come to visit you. You try to put them at ease with self-deprecating humor.

"I always thought the brain was like Jell-O, but it turns out it's more like Play-Doh."

"I need that like a hole in the head. Oh wait, never mind, I already have one."

But they still look sad coming in the door, and they try not to look sad when they're with you but you can tell they are, and they look sad going out the door.

You rarely cry in front of them, or anyone. You only cry at night, and not from despair, only from an awesome frustration at not having half of your body, and, perhaps, from shock. One day you're walking around, the next you can't sit up or roll over in bed. It is shocking. But it's just as shocking to your family. They are paralyzed, in their own way, along with you. They don't need to see tears. They need to hear you crack a joke. So you crack jokes for them.

"I always wanted to be right. Now, I'm nothing *but* right! I guess you can accuse me of being one-sided."

"I guess the only dancing I'll be doing is the sidestep."

You're going to be a better person. You know that is in fact true. That's the reason for all this. You're going to be a better person.

Since you don't cry when people can see you, the staff all think you don't actually realize what's happened to you.

Dr. Jerk gives you a lecture one morning. "You're going to need to cry," he tells you. "You should get some therapy so you can cry. You're in denial."

You say, "I'm not in denial. I'm just focusing on how I'm going to get out of here. I'm going to walk again. And I'm going to have another baby."

He looks at you for a long time. You don't think he can roll his eyes any farther back in his head. Then he leaves and you can see him out in the hall talking to Jim. The door is ajar but you can see his lips move. You watch his lips closely.

What is he saying? You follow the lips moving and finally put it together.

He is telling Jim, more or less, "She says she hasn't cried. That means she hasn't accepted what's happened yet. That's because she's in denial. She needs to resign herself to the fact that she can't have another baby. And if she lives, she may never walk again."

What does he know? Certainly not you. You know your body better than he would or could ever know it.

Trust your gut. That's your soul speaking. It doesn't lie. Intuition is only about truth.

THERE ARE TIMES THAT YOU LOSE the nurse-call button. Either you are lying on top of it, or you've let it fall to the side of the bed. It might as well be in Nicaragua. You are no longer capable of rolling over and picking it up. When this happens, it occurs to you that you're utterly helpless.

■　■　■

YOU HAVEN'T HAD A BOWEL MOVEMENT in nine days. The nursing staff has been pumping you with suppositories and stool softeners. Part of it is fear; you've been told not to do anything that may strain you or put pressure on your brain.

YOU HAVE PASSED OUT while being moved to the potty chair. Three nurses are hoisting you back on the bed. Your whole body is one massive shaking spasm. You must be having a seizure. You think, *Okay, tonight I'm going to die.*

"She's had a . . ."

You can't quite make out the words that come next, but they sound like "varsil-vegal." Whatever that is, you had one. It sounds like a forbidden word. Now that you've experienced it, you figure, whatever the hell it is, it should be taboo.

When it finally passes, and they've heaved you back onto your bed, you hear yourself say out loud, "I don't have a body anymore."

You hear yourself sob. The nurses try to console you. You know they mean well, but what can they possibly say to make you feel better? "At least you're alive"? Even that's questionable—no one is willing to tell you you'll survive this.

You are weeping for about fifteen minutes. A nurse stays with you. She's your age and she has a child about Rory's age. She's sad because you're sad.

You finally stop crying and say to her, "I'm not particularly crazy about this movie. I need you to rent another one for me, one with a happy ending."

"This is the only one we've got," she says, smiling a little. "But the ending is up to you."

DR. NEURO VISITS YOU on his morning rounds.

The story now looks like this: You had a horrific evening, suffering a "varsil-vagel" (or whatever the hell it's called) after completing a long-awaited bowel movement.

You say to him, "I finally had a bowel movement . . . after nine days!" You wait for pearls of wisdom to issue forth from the physician you have decided you like the best. He looks at you for a long time, clearly polishing something brilliant he has to say about your condition.

"It really stinks, doesn't it?" he asks, soberly.

You both crack up.

He's the one you trust—not only with your life but also, now, with your sanity.

EVERY DOCTOR IN THE HOSPITAL, it seems, is trying to diagnose you.

You are obviously of great interest to the neurology team. They're always materializing and vanishing. You frequently wake up to find yourself surrounded by residents with clipboards. One resident, tall with red hair and a bony face that reminds you of a skull, mentioned to you—yesterday? the day before? the week before?—that your condition has "become the subject of many heated debates."

"You're the reason the rounds take so long these days," he says, making a face at you. He seems to want it to be a joke.

"Hey," you say. "I don't want to be here either. At least I make the rounds interesting."

"Watch out." He grins. "This place may make you famous. You'll find yourself in some textbook if you're not careful."

DR. JERK, YOU CONCLUDE, has an overblown ego and an obnoxious bedside manner.

He insists you need a drug called Cytoxan in order to treat the vasculitis he has concluded you have.

He stands by your bed and squints through the baby fat. There is a younger doctor next to him, still as a ventriloquist's dummy, and with laminated hair too.

"CYTOXAN will probably make her STERILE," Dr. Jerk says, repeating the words slowly so they can't possibly be misunderstood. "But she's going to have to DO it anyway." He has been looking at his fellow doctor, the ventriloquist's dummy to whom he has, presumably, been speaking, but he pauses and turns his eyes to you to see if what he just said sank in.

Whenever he talks to you (or, in this case, around you), he speaks more loudly than he does to the nurses. It's as though he thinks sick people are stupid by nature. "Despite the fact that it will probably make her STERILE," he says, once more, still staring at you, "we're just going to have to DO it."

"No, it won't MAKE HER STERILE," you say.

"Why is that?" he asks, pen clutched between red fat fingers.

"Because I'm NOT GOING to DO it. And P.S., JULIA DOESN'T have vasculitis, EITHER."

You say your words slow and loud, just like he does.

"You just THINK she has vasculitis because that's what you KNOW about. You think EVERYONE has vasculitis. You probably think the TAPIOCA lady has vasculitis. Well, we've got NEWS for you. We DON'T all have vasculitis. Is it because you're so SHORT that you have to overcompensate by always proving yourself RIGHT? If you haven't made any mistakes, she DOESN'T think you're very smart."

You believe mistakes are a learning tool, and this is clearly a guy with a lot of tools to take advantage of.

He stares at you for a long time. He may not get the tapioca lady thing.

"You're in DENIAL," he pronounces slowly, as though he were talking to a very slow four-year-old. "There are going to be some SIDE EFFECTS. But don't worry. You have your SON. That's GOOD. You already HAVE a son. Anyway we're going to start treatment IMMEDIATELY. It's a PROPHYLACTIC."

He stares at you again to see if you've misunderstood the word. He would love you to misunderstand the word. He doesn't mean condoms. He means a kind of protection from the incurable disease he's so good at recognizing that he probably sees it in his breakfast cereal every morning.

"I . . . DON'T . . . HAVE . . . VASCULITIS," you say, slow and loud. "And I DON'T want to have chemo. And anyway I need a little TIME to PROCESS all this, okay?"

He points the tip of his ballpoint pen at you and leans in close.

"I'm GOING to TALK to your FAMILY about this," he says.

"YEAH? So what? I'M going to talk to my family about YOU."

AFTER DISCUSSING THIS with your family and in the glaring absence of any other diagnosis, Dr. Jerk wears you down and you agree to his course of treatment. There are many types of chemotherapy, and the one Dr. Jerk has prescribed for you requires at least eight hours of hydration.

Hydration, the nurses tell you, is basically having to pee for eight hours straight. This is one time when having a catheter attached to your bladder has its advantages. You need to be hydrated by an intravenous drip for four hours to protect your kidneys and liver. The poison is a forty-five-minute drip, and then you get another round of hydration. Otherwise, Cytoxan would do severe damage to your internal organs.

All your life you've been taking your vitamins and trying to eat from the right food groups. Now you're letting the nurses poison you. They may call it something different, but Cytoxan is a poison, and they are putting it in the intravenous line that has been surgically implanted on your left side below your shoulder. It goes against every instinct to allow them to put this poison into your body, but now you can't resist because you have to be strong for your family.

You are crying quietly. The nurse who is shooting you full of the stuff is old and jowly and has hair the color of iron and she can't be more than five foot two. She actually seems to be enjoying this. Nurse Doom.

You wish you could literally stick it to her.

Instead you tell her, "Look at me."

She stares up from the needle and looks at you.

"I am going to walk again. Do you hear me? After this is over, I am going to get better and walk again. And I am having another baby, goddammit."

You wait for her to change her expression, but she doesn't. She just looks at you for a minute, then looks down at the needle again, then looks over at the IV bag full of clear poison that is now rushing into your veins.

Chat with Nurse Doom

YOU ARE CRYING AS QUIETLY as you can and Nurse Doom is administering the IV.

"You know," she says in a low voice, staring at the needle, "there's a department here that can get special hats for chemotherapy patients."

Her job description must include speaking words of cheer to patients receiving injections of poison.

You glare at her angular face and cold blue eyes as you feel the stuff coursing through you. You find your eyes drawn to Nurse Doom's own stiff white trifold hat, which looks like something out of the 1940s.

"Is there a department," you ask, "for nurses' hats? Because I think you've *got* to update yours to this century."

She stiffens, but doesn't look at you.

"A lot of chemotherapy patients," she growls out slowly, "have problems adjusting afterward. A lot of chemotherapy patients are *glad* that there's a department that can get hats for them."

Silence. Neither of you wants to talk next.

You are a chemotherapy patient.

You conjure up a dunce cap in your mind.

To be honest, hair is the least of your worries at the moment. Half of your head is shaved flat and bald and embroidered with an intricate S-shape pattern of staples. The other half has shoulder-length hair and you can tell, even now, even without looking at it, that it is getting matted and gnarly. It hangs unevenly, and there's a strange weight to it.

Finally, she breaks the silence.

"There is a department that administers support groups for chemotherapy patients here. You're the sort of patient who should take advantage of that program."

The sort of patient who should take advantage.

You.

Not only a chemotherapy patient. But the sort who should take advantage. Great. Now you have another support group to attend. "I'm still working on trying to sit up," you tell her. "Is there a support group for how to deal with medical staff?"

She keeps staring at the needle. For some reason she doesn't want to look at you.

"I'm sorry I made fun of your hat."

No response.

"But I have to tell you it is still kind of weirding me out."

She coughs. On purpose. That little cough people cough that says, "That's enough."

She turns on her heel and her angular face vanishes. You hear the door close and the footsteps clicking away, quieter and quieter, down the hall until they're gone.

Nurse Doom has apparently had her fill of you.

You cry as loud as you want for a few minutes.

Then the room goes wobbly and things are bluer and colder. It's like ice being pushed through your veins, and you notice that the inside of your mouth tastes like pennies. And you make a mental note to yourself that it's time to get a haircut.

Eek! A Mouse

"ALL I'M SAYING is think about it."

For some reason your dad is really worked up about the decision to cut off the hair on the side of your head that isn't bald and glittering with staples and red puncture wounds.

He's there by your bed, just at the edge of your field of vision. By him is a table filled with flowers and a tiny man with a frizzy black halo of hair who keeps telling you his name, Curtis, and who is unpacking a beauty case. Your dad is making his trying-to-smile expression, which he's been doing a lot lately, and you're trying to talk yourself into eating a hot fudge sundae.

"All I'm saying is, it's a big step and why cut off your hair if you don't have to?"

You need help to eat everything, including this hot fudge sundae. Everything you eat tastes like pennies, not that you've ever eaten pennies, but it's what you imagine they taste like. You ask your dad to put it on the table next to your bed.

Useless.

"Don't you want to keep your hair?"

"Dad," you say, "I would if I had the other half. The half-bald look isn't in this year."

You look at Curtis.

"Let's get it over with."

He turns on a buzz cutter and runs it along the side of your head. It tickles. Five or six strokes. You feel it fall. Then Curtis gathers it up and shows it to you and gives you a little smile.

"Sinead O'Connor's got nothing on you, kid," Curtis says.

You stare at the small mop of hair he's removed from your head and is now extending toward you like a trophy. The weekend before your stroke, which now seems like a couple of centuries ago, you paid $140 to have that clump of hair styled, permed, and cut. Now it looks a little like a rodent in hibernation.

"Throw it away," says your dad.

"No," you tell Curtis. "Put it here on the bed."

Curtis does.

"Anything else?" Curtis asks.

"Yeah," you say. "Do you do nails?"

Curtis smiles.

"Of *course* I do nails."

"Good," you say. "Could you please do mine? Something bright. Unlike this room."

THAT NIGHT, WHEN YOU'RE all alone again, you toss the clump of hair on the floor in front of your bed and press the call button.

Quicker than you expect, a nurse materializes. She leans in the door halfway and says "Yeeeeess?" Plump, big eyes, blond hair, smile. It's Brenda. There are so many nurses to keep track of. You make a mental exercise of remembering as many of their names as possible. You even try to remember their kids' names. Brenda is usually willing to listen to you when you want to talk about the treatment or ask questions or pick up the TV remote. Brenda is your happy-go-lucky nurse.

You're glad it's Brenda who has materialized.

"There's a mouse in my room."

You try to show no emotion. You point at the floor.

She steps in the door and looks at the floor.

"Oh dear." Mock horror. "Better make a call."

It does look like a mouse down there, at least with only the hallway lights on.

"I think it's dead," you intone solemnly. "It wouldn't move when I yelled at it. Turn on the lights and see if it runs away."

She steps to the doorway and clicks the light. She stares at the clump of hair on the floor. Then she steps toward it cautiously. Then she leans down and looks at it closely.

"You," she says quietly, "are a troublemaker."

Still kneeling by what used to be your hair, she looks up at you. The minute you make eye contact, you both start laughing hard, right out loud.

It feels good. You both keep doing it for as long as the laugh can last.

Finally the laughter eases away into the distance, and she picks up the hair and throws it in the wastebasket.

She stands next to you and puts her hand on your shoulder.

"Did you have anything, you know, *real* to ask?"

You think for a moment.

"Yes," you say. "Yes, I do."

"What?"

You show her the fingernails on your right hand . . . *masterpieces*.

"Don't my nails look *fabulous*?" you ask.

Brenda is impressed, and she should be. Curtis spent over an hour and a half on them. The left hand wouldn't stay anywhere you put it. It was a major project.

"What do you think? Not your usual diva red, huh?" you ask.

THE CRITICAL CARE HOSPITAL nursing staff is a group of extremely caring individuals. The kindness is completely genuine. On Saturdays, Nurse Happy-Go-Lucky brings you fresh bagels and cream cheese. These are supposed to be for the nurses only, but she shares with you. It feels so good that she would do that.

You take a long look at the bagel with cream cheese. It occurs to you that you are very lucky to have it, very lucky to have a nurse like Brenda who will bring you something good to eat on a sunny morning like this—you're grateful for that, too. And for a heart beating inside your chest. Even with some things not working like they used to, even with half of your body gone, you're alive and there is a window, and luminous sun bouncing orange light off the wet street, and the city waking up and getting ready to go to work. But here you are watching it instead of driving southbound on Route 128 and someone you like just gave you a bagel. It's the best bagel in the world.

You are weeping, staring at the window, staring at the bagel, so grateful for it you don't want to spoil it by picking it up and eating it.

You need help. Chewing is difficult—you keep biting your tongue and cheek. Cream cheese must be all over your face. You don't care. You're supposed to be here. God wanted you to be here and receive food from someone who wanted to feed you something she was supposed to be eating but she gave it to you instead. God put you here. God kept the heart in your chest beating. God gave you this food through Nurse Happy-Go-Lucky.

So you could do something.

You don't really know what it is though.

Bring it on.

Don't Leave Me This Way

WHEN YOU WERE A KID, you thought riding in an ambulance would be exciting—going fast, passing all the other cars, sirens screaming. You never thought about the reasons that might make you a passenger in one. The child in you liked the idea of the frenzied activity, the urgency.

> *Mom driving all of you to swimming lessons, the wood-panel Country Squire station wagon, and an ambulance would shriek past you. Mom silenced everyone and told you all to pray a Hail Mary for the faceless, genderless occupant of the ambulance. You liked to think that your prayers gave the (presumably) dying person a fighting chance.*

Now it's your turn for someone to recite the Hail Mary for you. You are the injured stranger to your fellow commuters. The transport from critical care to the next leg of your journey, the rehabilitation hospital, is jolting. You can't hear any siren. Jim is following along behind—or so they keep assuring you.

The ambulance is sweltering. Your head and neck are damp with sweat. You are strapped on your back to a stiff, unforgiving

gurney. Your body feels every single bump in the road. It's excruciating. When the ambulance hits one of the many potholes, your
central nervous system rattles and explodes, your body gets in-
creasingly stiff, and you feel it trying to coil like a spring. But you're
tied down, so you can only feel stiffness and spasms. You hit another
pothole and the explosions and spasms start again. You wonder if
this is what rigor mortis is like.

When the ambulance finally arrives at its destination, you are
jostled out of your tiny moving torture chamber into a much larger
stationary torture chamber—the rehab hospital.

The critical care hospital was always extremely clean. The
floors gleamed, and the rooms were pristine and modern looking.
Even as they wheel you into this place, you can tell from the smell
of it and the look of the ceiling tiles that you are entering a place
that is old and worn out. You don't like it.

There are no rooms available on the neurology floor. Brain
trauma must be more popular than heart problems: They find you
an open room on the cardiac floor until a room in the neurology
unit opens up.

The emergency medical technicians bring you into a room
with two beds and a harsh fluorescent light that is oddly off
center. You are relieved that no one else is here to share the
space.

"Which bed would you like?"

"Neither. I want my own room."

The EMT, staring at you blankly, looks clueless.

"I'll take the upgrade—the one with the view by the
window."

No answer.

The EMTs are getting ready to leave. Jim is nowhere in
sight.

"Please," you say to them, before they vanish. "Don't."

One of the guys leaves, like you didn't say anything at all. But
the squat, pleasant-looking fellow who drove the ambulance through

every available pothole stops and turns to look at you. "Don't what?" he asks.

"Don't leave me here. It's a mistake, I'm not supposed to be here," you answer.

He looks at you like you're joking. But you're pretty sure you're not.

He's gone.

You're alone.

Click Your Heels Three Times
and Press the Call Button

IN ADDITION TO THE MISPLACED lighting fixture, the room has putrid mint green walls and an exhausted pink linoleum floor.

The bed on which you have been placed boasts a thin, sagging mattress covered by two threadbare sheets that now envelop you carelessly. It is late July, and even at dusk, the room is broiling.

You press the call button. A black box above your head crackles loudly.

A voice buzzes: "What do you need?"

"It's really hot."

The voice buzzes again: "Sorry. Can't change it."

One stroke isn't enough, now you're going to have another—a heat stroke. You press the call button again.

The black box squawks: "Yes."

You shout, "Is this purgatory or hell? Or are you the Wizard of Oz in there, in that speaking box? And if you're the Great Oz, I want to go *home*."

Silence.

You weep. Time passes. You have no idea how much of it, but it passes.

When an aide arrives at your bedside, you say, "I was beginning to think humans didn't really work here. What do you think of cranking the air conditioner up a notch, please?"

In a robot move she turns her back to you. You think she must be adjusting some settings somewhere, but instead she opens up the window. Yeah, that's just what you needed. Now you can smell the auto exhaust, hear the road rage of the southeast expressway, and still be just as hot.

"You should have someone bring you a fan, because that's how patients deal with the heat here."

"What? Have somebody bring in a fan for me—you're kidding, right? What is this, a hospital or a homeless shelter? This place charges more per day than the Ritz-Carlton and you're telling me you have no way to control the temperature?"

The aide leaves.

Jim still isn't here. Maybe they were lying about him following the ambulance after all.

It's you and the black box. Period.

You press the call button.

Nothing happens.

You glare at the black box. You press the call button again.

Silence.

Empty hall.

So much for the orientation process at this hospital. Patient care resides in a little black box over your head.

TWO WEEKS EARLIER, you had been power walking, managing multiple projects, and performing a dizzying variety of physical and mental tasks. Now it's two in the morning and you're sprawled in a heap, kissing the foul, deadly pink linoleum floor in a rehab hospital.

Why did this happen? If you think hard, you are pretty sure you can reassemble this sequence of events. Got it—it happened because during a potty transfer, you leaned forward to take a sip of water from a cup that was directly in front of you. The floor is furious; your face aches from it. And now, as you lie in a pile on the floor, the aide is reprimanding you, too.

"That was *impulsive*," says the aide.

"No," you say, "that wasn't impulsive."

"Whatever," says the aide.

"Fuck you *sideways*," you say, biting off the words, with your mouth pressed against the floor. "Pick me *up*."

"I *beg* your pardon," says the aide.

"Now *that*," you say, pronouncing from the floor as clearly and carefully as you can, "*that* was impulsive. Trying to lean forward to get a drink of water, that's not impulsive. But saying 'Fuck you sideways' because you won't pick me up, *that's* impulsive. See? There's a difference."

YOUR BODY'S CENTER OF GRAVITY is something you never gave much thought to before. The brain does many things unconsciously, things like breathing—and stabilizing itself when you lean forward to get a drink of water. The brain's the boss, supposedly. Currently though, some of your body parts are guilty of insubordination.

In fact, the entire left side of your body now refuses to take orders from the boss. No one on the left side is listening—they've quit their jobs. So the boss has pretty much chosen to ignore the left side of your body. It no longer exists, according to your brain.

THE FALL HAPPENED at a little before two in the morning; there was only one aide to hoist you from the bed to the potty chair next to your pathetic, sagging bed. You required two—it was a matter of policy. Down you went. There followed a full-body X-ray in your bed. Your shoulder shows a two-inch separation between your limb and your shoulder joint.

The aide says it's because of your fall—and the fact that you're "impulsive."

Actually, it's from her yanking your arm to get you back up off the floor.

You're starting to see a pattern here: The bigger the staff's error, the more "impulsive" you are.

"It's typical for right-hemisphere strokes to act impulsive," says the doctor who takes the x-rays.

You may be brain damaged, but you know full well they're just covering their asses. It's an unspoken rule: Always find a reason to blame the patient for any problem. This reduces the risk of lawsuits.

Two weeks ago you were in charge of your life. Now that misplaced fluorescent light above you seems to be running things.

You can still hear the surly aide's verdict in your head: "That was impulsive."

You press down on the call box button for at least a minute and hear yourself weeping when someone finally answers.

Impulsively Yours

THE VERY SAME AIDE REMATERIALIZES bearing a disgusting-looking tuna sandwich. You ignore it. She asks you what's wrong.

"You really want to know?"

"Of course."

So you tell her.

"My husband isn't here. My brain, which has allowed me to be an independent human being for thirty-seven years or so, has decided to go on strike. I never had to think about each individual instruction the brain gives my limbs in order for me to walk or sit up erect in a chair. I'm not impulsive. I have never suffered from denial. My brain is just getting caught up to the fact that half of me is paralyzed and must be moved with conscious thought. Also, people don't answer when I press the call button, or if they do, they sound like the guy behind the curtain in the *Wizard of Oz*. And this room is really freaking me out. It's purgatory. Just looking at the pink of that floor makes me nauseous. And I don't much care for the smell of the place. And I wouldn't feed that tuna sandwich to a stray cat. That's what's wrong."

She frowns.

"Toto," you say in a mock whisper, "we're not in Kansas anymore. Can you please try to find me something else to eat?"

"Can't. The cafeteria's closed."

"Okay. Let me get this straight. Food of any kind, other than that tuna sandwich you've got there, is not an option until the cafeteria opens for breakfast? Is that what you're telling me?"

She writes something on your clipboard.

Probably the word "impulsive."

"WE'RE CONCERNED ABOUT your outlook." A coven of doctors around your bed staring at you. Now you're supposed to say something.

"That's a coincidence. I'm concerned about *your* outlook."

"The aides say things haven't been going well. It says here that you're impulsive."

The doctor who is talking is a large misshapen man with a ponytail, a pink face, and the inevitable clipboard.

"Were you impulsive *before* this happened to you?"

You look at him squarely and say, "If you mean impulsive like buying something extraordinary that I didn't need in the flash of a moment, then yes. If you are saying impulsive as in a danger to society, no."

He nods sagely.

"Anything you'd like to add?"

"Yeah. I'm not lashing out because of what happened to me, and I'm not in denial. I just don't like this place. It has to be the single most depressing room I've ever been in in my life. And P.S., if not liking the linoleum is a reason to reprimand me, even though I had an up-close and personal meeting with it, then I think we should also be talking to somebody else about a reprimand for the color choices in here."

"Is that it?"

"No. That's not it. Isn't this a place where people come to get help *recovering* from whatever has, you know, befallen them? If that's so, then why does everyone act like I'm an inconvenience? Or a description? Or a line on a chart? I need positive interactions. All I've gotten here is negativity."

Impulsive.

You hate goddamn labels.

Which Hand Was That?

IT MUST BE MORNING BECAUSE sunlight is coming through the window in greasy streaks. A man in a white coat is looming over your bed.

"I'm your physiatrist."

"Why do I need a psychiatrist? I thought I was doing pretty well handling this."

"I'm not a psychiatrist. I'm a physiatrist."

"What the hell is that? I've never heard of that specialty before."

"I'm the doctor responsible for your overall rehabilitation. When you're done with the critical care doctors and stabilized enough to work on your rehabilitation. It's the 'physical' recovery we work on here."

Your physiatrist is a little elflike man who has curly black hair and a tendency to look at you the way a keeper looks at an animal in the zoo. When he scrunches up his nose he reminds you a little of Peter Rabbit.

Dr. Bleak.

"Touch your thumb to each finger separately," he says, nose squinched.

You touch your thumb to your finger. No problem: Your fingers are quick and agile.

"That was easy," you say triumphantly.

"Not your *right* hand," Dr. Bleak complains, agitated. "Your *left* hand."

Oh.

He wants you to do the same trick with your left hand. The one that isn't really there. The one that's a faraway radio station your brain can't seem to tune in to.

You try. Nothing. Your arm doesn't even move. It lies on the bed, dead.

"Is that bad?" you ask.

"Only if you plan to use the hand again," he says, then flashes a tight little smile. "Seriously, if you can't do it now, you won't ever be able to do it. You should probably get used to that idea."

Nice way to squelch a little thing called hope, you think. The doctors here seem to specialize in identifying ideas you ought to get used to.

He writes something on his clipboard. You try to read upside down—something you used to be able to do—but you can't. Written words don't make sense. The hundreds of cards you receive don't make sense. You simply can't read, at least not more than a stray word here and there. Your left-side neglect removes all the letters on the left side of the page.

You manage to pick up a single word from the clipboard: "Denial."

You picture yourself using your nonexistent left hand to flip him the bird.

Everyone needs a goal. For now, that one is yours.

With Apologies to David Letterman

The Top Ten List of Post-Stroke Indignities—Institutional Edition

10. LOSING TRACK OF YOUR LIMBS. Your hand and arm have become appendages that are more like pieces of luggage that you have to lug around. One evening, while you were positioned on your left side, you lay facing your mother as she sat in a chair next to you. You had been talking normally when you suddenly panicked because you didn't know where your arm was. Your eyes wide, you said to her, "Where is my arm? I lost my arm!" As though it had walked out and had gone down to the cafeteria for a cup of coffee without you.

9. BEING VELCROED INTO PLACE. The therapist built a special tray for the wheelchair that your arm can be Velcroed onto. This prevents your arm from falling into the spokes of the wheelchair and getting tangled up in the works, or jamming into doorways during tight entries. Both problems have arisen repeatedly.

8. HAVING TO BE MOVED TO AND FROM the portable toilet chair by total strangers who have to hold you as you defecate. It's amazing how much autonomy is based on being able to go to the bathroom on your own. Back to potty training at age thirty-seven!

7. REGULARLY HAVING TO *REQUEST* that a pair of total strangers be summoned to move you to and from the toilet. You are a two-person job.

6. HAVING YOUR ASS WIPED BY SOMEONE ELSE. When you made your list of New Year's resolutions last December, being able to handle personal cleansing tasks you thought you had mastered at age three was definitely *not* what you envisioned on your list of things to be accomplished. Yet it has, amazingly, become a major life goal, almost as important as the goal of being able to flip the bird to certain members of the medical establishment.

5. SLIDING OFF A CHAIR WITHOUT MEANING TO when your center of gravity shifts. Your flesh has become Jell-O.

4. HITTING THE WALL with the back of your head before you land in a heap on the floor.

3. MAKING A SOUND UPON IMPACT that makes someone else run in from another room.

2. BEING REQUIRED TO WEAR A LEG-FOOT SPLINT, as well as a hand-arm splint, and a wedge to keep your shoulder in its socket.

And the number one post-stroke indignity is . . . *(Drum roll)*

1. LISTENING TO PEOPLE SPEAK ABOUT YOU as though you are not in the room.

Case in Point

TWO MORE WHITE COATS, talking to a blue jumper. One of the white coats is clutching that ubiquitous clipboard. The three of them are about eight feet away from you, but it feels like a mile and a half.

"How is she doing?"

"Well, to tell you the truth . . ."

"What?"

"It's going to be tricky."

"How do you mean?"

"She's lost a lot of real estate. She's always going to be . . ." (*Inaudible*)

"Yeah, but it's more than that."

"More?"

"She's in serious denial."

"Get a psych consult."

Cry Me a River

DR. BLEAK, YOUR ASSIGNED PHYSIATRIST, continuously reinforces the idea that you're in denial. He hasn't seen you crying yet, so that's his proof. No crying equals you're in denial.

"You know," he says, "it would really help you in your recovery if you stopped blocking the facts and accepted the reality of what has happened to you. Please consider attending the stroke support group here on this floor to help you accept your condition."

Marie, a close friend of yours from work, visits you regularly. She too is concerned that you're not aware of what has happened. "Julia, I can't help noticing that you're always joking and laughing. It's okay to cry. You can cry to me. It'd be good for you."

But you know full well what has happened, at least, you know as much as anyone else does. You had a stroke. The effects are severe. Beyond that you choose simply to pose questions rather than make statements. They're scary, but if you were in denial you wouldn't be able to pose them at all.

Do you truly have a life-altering incurable disease like cerebral vasculitis? Will the vessels in your head start to bleed spontaneously someday? Will you have another stroke? Will you die soon? Will you be able to return home, raise your child, have any independence? Will your husband become a caregiver and feel stuck in the marriage? Will your arm ever work well enough to pick your little boy up or bear-hug your husband again? Will you ever work again? Are you done being a mother?

There are so many things you could be terrified of if you choose to. You are already physically crippled. You can't paralyze yourself any further by freezing up emotionally. Your attitude is the only control you have left in your life—that and your nail polish color, of course.

You don't want to be the recipient of people's pity, nor do you want to deal with their sadness. The solution is to always joke in a self-deprecating way. The best medicine, you decide, is a room full of laughter. Laughter helps you improve every day. There are times you have so many people in your room, it feels like a private party. People are lying on the bed with you, sitting on the floor with you, cramming their chairs into the room. You almost forget where you are.

Almost. But not quite.

If laughter is the best medicine, why do you still hurt?

Just having a *goal* doesn't mean you're in denial. It means you're alive. Your goal is to return to the person you were prior to the stroke. Maybe somebody else would feel it's unrealistic. Maybe somebody else would feel it's ridiculous. But it's a goal. It's better than giving up. And it's a sign that you understand what has happened to you well enough to respond to it constructively.

EVERY TIME DR. BLEAK makes his rounds, he asks, "Did you go to the stroke support meeting?"

"Is there anybody like me there?" you ask. "Is there anybody who is thirty-seven years old who has a three-year-old child? I would like to know if there is anyone who mirrors me there, anyone I can identify with." You know most people who suffer from stroke are twice your age. It's a convenient way of changing the subject.

The floor counselor and a few of the nurses also drop hints

that you ought to go. It's as if they all think your attending these meetings would make you realize you had a stroke. Then you'd cry in front of them, and they could check you off some list.

IT'S NOT THAT YOU DON'T EVER CRY. You just do it in private. You cry fairly regularly, because the injury is not yours alone but also that of everyone who loves you. They are suffering as well. But crying in public is just too painful, and you know it would be hard on your family.

So the crying happens on your own. You stop in at a private "pity party" now and then, but you always know when it's time to leave.

AFTER ONE OF MARIE'S VISITS where she encourages you to cry, you decide, "All right, I'm going to try Marie's method and cry and feel hopelessly sorry for myself." The end result gives you a stuffed nose and a pounding headache, and you feel like a dishrag the entire next day. It really sucks. This is not the route you want to travel for your recovery.

Dr. Bleak, making his usual morning rounds, is surprised to find you sad and congested from crying. He says, "You seem to be depressed. You really should attend the stroke support group." Now he had switched "D" words on you. Tears? You're depressed! No tears? You're in denial. It must be wonderful to be God, tossing those labels around and making people believe them.

MORE OUT OF EXHAUSTION than anything else, and a deep-seated desire to move on to another topic of conversation with Dr. Bleak, you go to the next support meeting. There are three other patients and a counselor in a lounge area. The other patients in the meeting are all men: one in his early seventies who was recovering from his second stroke, a young man in his late twenties who was an immigrant from Jamaica, and a man in his forties.

The counselor doesn't counsel much, but instead demands that each person take a turn speaking. The man in his seventies speaks of his fear and anxiety that a stroke will happen to him again. The young Jamaican talks about who will take care of him once he is released. His family is spread in different locations, with his sister in Florida being the closest relative.

The man in his forties is extremely angry. He suffered seizures regularly prior to his stroke, and he had arranged to have a certain risky type of surgery to calm his seizures. When he awoke from his surgery he discovered that he had had a stroke, which his doctors warned him could happen. Now he is absolutely livid about his condition.

You find you have no patience for his "why me" attitude. Every patient in this hospital could adopt the same mind-set and make the same complaints. Did his way of thinking help him? No. It was simply a delusion, a cheap way for him to imagine that he was somehow superior to everyone else in the building.

"I'm going to sue the doctor for doing this to me," he says.

"Weren't you told of the risks prior to the surgery?" you ask.

He screams his answer: "I signed some documents saying I understood the risks, but I didn't think it was actually going to happen to *me!*"

This guy is really getting on your nerves.

"Listen," you say, "you have got to stop looking around and blaming everybody. Start looking at *yourself* and saying, 'Hey, I am going to get myself better. I am not going to put up with this condition.' Take all your negative energy and put it toward recovery instead of wasting it by pointing at everyone else. Because in the end, you're still going to be in the same condition—unless *you* do something about it. There's a Chinese saying I heard once: 'Hatred does more damage to the vessel it is contained in than the vessel it is directed at.' Focus within yourself and you'll have a better chance for recovery and a better life."

The stroke counselor is so pleased with your little speech that she asks you to come again and be a group leader. This surprises you because, physically at least, you are in worse shape than your counterparts. You expect a group leader to be someone who has actually made some kind of tangible progress.

You decline the offer because you don't want to belong to a group that makes pity parties a part of the routine. You won't allow yourself to bemoan your own fate, and you know you will have a hard time listening to the inevitable whining and rage that will come from other patients. Plus there's a lot of talk about setting and discussing individual goals as part of the group's activity. You refuse to accept anyone's idea of what your goals should be. Goal setting, you realize, is a personal matter.

Facing the Chicken

IT'S YOUR FIRST SUNDAY EVENING AT REHAB, and Mom and Dad are visiting. Dad likes to have missions, and he can see that food is going to be a problem. He goes to Davio's in Cambridge, an upscale restaurant where takeout is not an option. He sits down and looks at the menu and orders the roasted halibut with black bean and mango salsa and says, "Make it ready to go."

They don't do ready to go.

To get the order, he tells a sob story—one that's true and has you as the lead character. The waitress relates her own story to him: It turns out she had a serious accident and was badly disabled for a while. She was in the hospital for six months. Dad is psyched to see that it is possible to overcome devastating injuries. Here she is a waitress, someone with a physically demanding job. He returns to your room all excited: "I just met somebody who was injured and couldn't walk but now is walking and working." You know it's a brass ring he's putting out there for you, but it's also one for him, too. He's having difficulty dealing with your injury and doesn't know how to express it.

YOUR BROTHERS BRING YOU LUNCH AND DINNER for the two months that you are in rehab. They organize a weekly calendar in which each brother is responsible for a certain time slot. You'd get the daily call from the Responsible Brother for that day.

"What do you feel like?" asks your brother John.

"Can I have anything I want?"

"Anything."

"How about Chinese without the chopsticks?"

"Really?"

"Really. I can barely handle a fork, really."

"What kind of Chinese?"

"Whatever is easiest for you to pick up. Just make sure you get a few fortune cookies—I could use some good insights in bed."

Your eldest brother, Jimmy, does his service on Friday nights, and he prefers to bring swordfish kebabs on rice with salad, and a blondie for dessert. He knows that you like it, so that's what you got every Friday night.

John has Tuesdays. Sometimes John would bring his own favorite, caesar salad with grilled chicken. Joe brings pizza from Fig's, a local pizza joint. It's always half eaten by the time it gets to you.

"The smell got to me and I was hungry," Joe says.

Jerry always brings a loaded tuna sandwich and fruit salad. Justin always brings lobster-salad rolls.

Jeffrey would travel over an hour to visit. He'd bring you a loaded sub and, although it was messy, he'd pick up the stray shreds of lettuce and diced tomatoes and help you get most of it in your mouth and not on your lap. "I love the smell of a sub when I'm starving," you say. "I just hate the smell after I've devoured it."

Your brother Tommy calls you one day and says, "I'm going to bring you some home cooking; it's going to be a surprise." He arrives that evening with a roasted chicken on the bone.

Now the rule is, supposedly, whoever brings the meal stays and helps you eat it. This is important because you have difficulty sitting up and even more difficulty eating one-handed. You also have to be monitored closely because you can choke easily. Tommy has to drop and run because that's the way he is, off to another important meeting. He's always on the go.

You had begged Jim to stay home that day because he was running ragged coming to the hospital every evening and most lunchtimes.

And Tommy just left.

So you're all alone.

It's you and the chicken.

You stare at it. You're starving. It looks delicious. And you have absolutely no idea what to do with it.

Hell, it's dinnertime. You're going to eat this damn bird.

You have some useless plastic utensils. You ponder why they even bother with plastic knives. "Self," you think, "figure it out."

You do a face plant on the roast chicken and start gnawing it like an animal. You know you look disgusting, but you don't really care. You're hungry.

Unbeknown to you, Jim has been standing at the doorway watching his lovely wife reduced to gnawing away at a carcass, like a fox in the pack. You both have a good belly laugh over this.

"There are going to be a lot of weird images of me, honey," you say as Jim cuts the chicken into pieces for you. "Images of me coping with my situation, images that I want you to erase from your memory banks. This is one of them!"

YOUR DOCTORS HAVE A CAFFEINE RESTRICTION on your chart. You think it includes chocolate. This was a self-imposed rule because none of your doctors restricted chocolate. You love chocolate with every cell in your body.

Eating chocolate is sometimes like sex. It feels great and you always want more. The day Jimmy brought you your first post-stroke blondie bar you were uncertain about eating it. But there's an important moral principle at stake here: One should never be timid when it comes to chocolate.

The urge to have a piece of chocolate is greater than the fear of death. It's only a few chocolate chips, and after all, it's *blond* chocolate. You nibble and then wait, anticipating an explosion in your head. No trauma occurs, other than the realization that you can still eat chocolate and your hips can still expand.

PEOPLE YOU'VE WORKED WITH often bring lunches. Yoshi, a coworker who handled the Japanese products at your company, visits often. He always brings you something interesting from his culture. One of these was a little plaster doll with blank eyes. He explains that it symbolizes a goal. You color in a black spot on one blank eye while setting the goal you want to achieve. When you have reached your goal you color in the other eye.

Yoshi explains that the doll represents a proverb: "Fall down seven times, get up eight times."

"It's pretty obvious what my goal will be," you say, catching a glimpse of yourself in the mirror. "I want to be a glamorous Hollywood movie star."

He laughs. You stare at that lifeless, blank doll and then color in the right eye, resolving to heal your broken body.

The next time he brings you the most beautiful candy from Chinatown. Each piece is a work of art. They could have been glued in a frame. You don't want to eat them because they're so pretty, but then you decide to go for it. You take a big bite, expecting the beauty of the candy to enchant your tongue.

It doesn't.

"What is it?" you ask as you try to think of a way to spit it out without hurting his feelings. Yoshi says, "It's bean paste." As soon as he says that, you don't care about feelings. You only care about saving your taste buds from this foul trickery. You blast it right into a napkin.

After that episode, you enjoy offering this oriental "confection" to your guests.

YOUR FOLKS FILL ANY GAPS in the meal schedule. Dad brings you many meals. He calls too and says, "What do you feel like?" Then he goes to the pub below his office. You know he enjoys picking out your meals, because he orders all the things he enjoys but shouldn't eat. Sometimes he brings elaborate meals and other times it's something simple, like a burger and fries. Sometimes you're so hungry, you'll eat anything.

Except bean paste.

JASON, YOUR YOUNGEST BROTHER, doesn't bring you meals. Instead, he brings you a steady diet of humor. He usually brings his milky morning beer breath too, while describing his single-life escapades. The rehab hospital is, conveniently enough, right next to the T station which is J.V.'s primary means of transportation. He is living at home with the folks in Andover while completing law school. On weekends he comes into Boston. He hangs out with his buddies, and then he strolls into your room on a Saturday or Sunday morning all ratty looking. Sometimes you get his funny visits coming and going.

You call him Bubbalubba. He describes his personal dating scene. One date he knew had ended early because he saw her slip out a side door with another guy. Once, you ask him what happened to the woman who had achieved girlfriend status (because he had more than one date with her).

He says, "I think we broke up."

"Really? Why?"

"Because she had a party and didn't invite me."

Apparently she didn't know she had a boyfriend.

The support system seems infinite. Between family and friends, you're taken care of. One friend brought your absolute favorite chocolates, Stowaway Sweets. Not as pretty as the flower candy Yoshi brought, but it's edible. And it's real chocolate! To keep yourself in check, you make Jim keep the box out of reach and out of sight ("Put it on my left side") and dole out two or three onto a tray before he leaves. You savor those chocolates every night and feel like a princess as you do.

You want to make sure that you don't have any visitors who have a "pity attitude." You don't want the negative comments: "Oh I can't believe this happened to you, Julia." You want to keep your-self—and everyone else who crosses your threshold—positive. It's a form of protection. Jim spreads the word. Your close friends understand.

Mom is in the room when Jim is working. Mom oversees the meal and visitor schedule. If you don't have a lunch coming in with your brothers or friends, she's there with a home-cooked meal—and it is never roast chicken on the bone! She is always mothering: straightening and cleaning the room, bringing in necessities, laundering your clothes, taking clothes home, washing them, folding them, putting them back, hanging cards, putting pictures up—you really appreciate her efforts. You know she has suffered, seeing her only daughter in this condition. You know that, for you, it would be agonizing to watch someone you love being in this devastating and uncertain condition. You're relieved that you're the patient, and not the visitor.

You spend a lot of time pondering why someone staying in the hospital is called a "patient." Eventually, you come to a true under-standing of the term. You have always had a very impatient person-ality, whether the problem is sitting in traffic, expecting someone to arrive for an appointment, or waiting for anything. In the hospital, though, you have to learn to be patient for someone to answer the call light, to help you go to the bathroom, to get something for you that is out of your reach.

You learn to be patient about everything.

You also have to be patient for your body to heal.

Your belief is that people who are truly patient live longer. In our society we are taught to do everything expeditiously. When you enter a hospital as a patient, you need to make patience a part of your anatomy.

Who's Squinting?

Edie made bumpers for Rory's crib. Edie said, "These are for Rory's crib, and you can use them for all your children if you want. The color scheme works for a boy and it works for a girl, so you can use it for your next baby, too."

That's what Edie said to you.

"I'M STILL GOING TO HAVE A BABY. Right, Jim? Hop on, let's make one right now. " Your speech is slurred and sarcastic.

Every day, it seems, people arrive and kneel by your bedside. The room is overflowing with flower arrangements. It gives you the feeling that you're awake at your own wake.

Today Jim and your parents are kneeling at your bedside—Jim on one side, Mom and Dad on the other side.

You think it must be because they like to get eye to eye with you, so it's okay. You're all for that. If they want to kneel, let them kneel.

"Stop squinting," Dad says, as if it was a helpful instruction.

"I'm not squinting," you bark back.

"Yes, you are." It's like two kids bickering.

"Give me a mirror," you demand.

He does.

"There, see?" He's defiant.

The face in the mirror looks different than the one you re-membered. The shaved scalp has shifted everything, and there are strange new hairs in unbecoming places. Your overall countenance is bloated. The eyes of the reflection are foreign and asymmetrical. The left eye remains wide open with a blank stare. The right eye is in fact squinting. But that's only because it's doing what it's sup-posed to do—reacting to light and showing expression.

You stare at the eyes in the mirror and notice that tears are welling up in both of them.

You are still going to have a baby, though.

Dr. Neuro has put you on some prenatal vitamins. Jim squeezes your hand through the aluminum bars on the side of the bed, and suddenly it's okay that your mouth tastes like pennies and your head has a long raw scar and tiny metal ridges along the side of it and they keep telling you that you have something you *know* you don't have but you have no idea why you know that.

It's going to be okay. Everything really is eventually going to be okay.

Time wobbles again and your hand is through the aluminum bars, but Jim's isn't holding it anymore and no one is kneeling by your bed now, so it's later.

Brace Yourself

ON ONE OF YOUR OUTINGS, you meet a little boy about seven years old being escorted around the ward by two therapists. He wears a bicycle helmet that protects his head and a leg brace similar to yours. He looks sad.

You have your therapist wheel you over to him and then ask both the therapists if you can chat with him privately.

HE HAD FALLEN OUT of a window and sustained a head injury that restricted his leg movement. He's been a patient for several months. You feel for him.

"I understand how hard it is to be in the hospital when it isn't what you had planned," you say. "And I know what it's like to miss your family and your home." You point to your leg.

"Take a look at my brace."

He does.

"It's just like mine," he says.

"Things happen out of the blue," you say. "Only really smart people know this. People who aren't so smart *think* things don't happen out of the blue. They *think* nothing important can happen to you without you expecting it. But they're wrong. You and I know. Right?"

He nods.

"You and I are going to have to work really hard not to have to wear a leg brace down the road," you say. "But for now, it's a good thing we've got them, because they're helping us to move around, and we can't learn if we don't move around, right?"

"Right."

You have this urge to reach over and hug him. But he hugs you first.

NOBODY EVER SEEMS to give *you* a pep talk. People who are sent to work with you are always concentrating on you adapting to your new crippled body and telling you how you need to accept it.

As they're walking out the door after a session, they say, within your earshot, "She's in denial."

You say, loud enough for them to hear, "I can't wait to get back to my yard to play soccer with my son."

Numbness Is in the
Eye of the Beholder

ONE MORNING YOU ASK your mother about the profusion of greeting cards in your room. She reminds you that Paul, your colleague from work, has sent you a card every single day you were hospitalized.

You ask her to bring the pile of cards over to you. You look through them. They are all dated. They are all different. He has never duplicated a card. Some days, you realize, you've received more than one card from him. He will have to start making his own cards soon, you think, because before too long, he will have used up every get-well card that ever existed.

You choose one of the cards at random and open it up. Paul has written on it, "Every day aboveground is extra."

YOU DECIDE THAT APPEARANCE is important for someone who is overcoming a debilitation. Appearance sets your frame of mind.

You decide to feel good about yourself. You make sure you put your makeup on every day. Some of the staff think it's funny. Your left side is completely paralyzed, your arm hangs like a dead tree limb after a storm, but there you are, holding cosmetic lids with your mouth. You put eye makeup and lipstick on every morning after your shower.

Putting on lipstick or eyeliner on the left side of your face usually produces a look that reminds you of a five-year-old girl getting caught playing with Mommy's makeup. Your face is numb and there isn't any muscle tone. It's like putting on lipstick after a few shots of novocaine. What a mess.

You are going to do whatever it takes to feel good. If that means tricking yourself by using makeup, so be it. Whenever you have felt ugly in your life, you have always had an ugly day. Now you are putting on your makeup each day as though you were going onstage. You are acting, and the stage is life. You have had good days and bad days. You know that much. A positive appearance, you have decided, will help with the attitude.

Putting on makeup also gives you the chance to practice facial exercises. This is important, because the left side of your face is flaccid.

Paul teases you about your cosmetics: "She says, 'Oh, I'm paralyzed, can't do a damn thing.' But hand her a cosmetics bag and she's off and running!"

He's right, of course. Makeup motivates you. You realize that, as part of your cosmetics routine, you would pay very close attention to the people who speak to you.

Whenever a nurse would talk, you'd look very closely at her face, and realize that her whole face, not just her mouth, was speaking. Her eyebrows, her eyes, her forehead—all moving in harmony, all working together in a seamless way that most people hardly notice, take for granted, and engage in hundreds of times a day without a thought.

When you demand a mirror and speak into it, you see that your right eye squints and is expressive while the left eye remains wide open, without any movement. The right eyebrow moves up and down; the left eyebrow is flatlined. The left side of the mouth is paralyzed and the tongue and gums on that side are numb. When the face in the mirror speaks, half of it is saying, "I'm not really here." It looks disturbing.

So after the makeup you always exercise in front of the little mirror on your bed tray. You work on forming words, on smiling, and on eye expression.

"Mirror, mirror on the wall," you hear yourself say to the little mirror one morning, "who's the toughest of them all?"

As if in response, the madwoman down the hall wails a long howl, then starts to sob uncontrollably.

WHEN YOU WERE GROWING UP in a household of eight brothers (and two male dogs!), you often joked to your mom that there was too much testosterone in the house and that you needed to inject more estrogen in the atmosphere. Mom would roll her eyes and say, "You're impossible. Where did you come from?" Now, on a visit to the hospital, your brother Joe reminisces about when you were young and wanted to prove that you were as tough as the boys.

"You sat yourself down in the kitchen," Joe says, "put your elbow on the table, and said, 'Okay, wimps, who wants to be embarrassed by being beaten in arm wrestling by a girl?' And you proceeded to beat two brothers—and came close to beating me! You're strong, Julia. You're going to beat this. Only difference is, now you're wrestling with yourself."

The Babe

THERE'S A KNOCK ON YOUR DOOR and Mom opens it. It's Berkeley, clutching a life-size cardboard figure of Babe Ruth. It's the same Babe you had purchased for the company kickoff meeting . . . except with a few changes.

This Babe is adorned with tacky dangling earrings, a phone headset, a company logo baseball cap, and (what your mom notices first) a bulging jockstrap. There are signatures from everyone in the department. Berkeley explains that the earrings are because you love jewels, the headset represents what your department does, and the jock strap is a candy holder—for a vast store of Hershey's Kisses. You always kept a chocolate jar on your desk for anyone who needed a chocolate fix—usually Berkeley. Now he's returning the favor.

"How did you manage to carry it across the parking lot and up the elevator?" you ask, laughing. "People must have thought you were whacked. Did anyone say anything to you?"

"No, but a lot of people stared. I think they were trying to figure it out. Could I have a piece of chocolate?"

"Sure, help yourself. Maybe people think you're bringing it to a Red Sox player who's recuperating. You know—that whole Boston

Curse thing. I can't wait to start offering kisses to the nurses. If they look perplexed, I'll point to the jockstrap."

You love the whole idea—and you love Berkeley for making you laugh.

"Put Babe in the corner so when a nurse comes in, she'll think there's someone lurking in the room. I can't wait for the reaction."

He does. He sits on the side of the bed. You wait there together for your first victim.

"Thanks, Berkeley," you say. "Now, with the Babe on hand, I'll always have company!"

Kisses in a jockstrap—pretty perverted. But I wouldn't expect anything else from him. People are mortified when they walk in the room. It's the goof that keeps on goofing.

Your Friend Pays a Visit

EVERYTHING IS ABNORMAL after your stroke, but your period, it turns out, is still as regular as clockwork. Lucky you.

The huge black nurse is cleaning you up. She has just placed a call requesting a diaper. Your heart freezes.

So it's come to this.

She stands and throws a now-crimson washcloth in the plastic hamper.

"Do me a favor," you say. "Take a look at my chart. Tell me how old I am."

She stops in place, considers you for a moment, then goes to your chart.

"It says here you're thirty-seven, honey."

"That's what I thought. It doesn't say I'm eighty-four, does it?"

"No, dear—thirty-seven."

"And it definitely doesn't say that I'm six fucking months old, does it?"

She makes a little pout and squints at you.

"Yes, I'm thirty-seven years old. And I'm not going to wear a diaper. Please get me tampons from supplies."

"This is all the hospital has."

"Are you serious? Is this some kind of joke you people play with the folks on the head-case floor? What the hell do other women do when they menstruate while they're in the hospital?"

"The hospital just doesn't supply tampons. We don't have napkins either."

"Well, I'm not in a coma. I'm coherent. I may lose track of time, and I may not be able to read very well, but I'm *not* wearing a fucking diaper, and I guarantee you anybody who tries to make me wear one is going to have a bad day. Please call my husband and ask him to bring me tampons. He'll help me. You won't have to do a thing."

She does.

ON THE WEEKEND, they suggest that you get out for a "walk" with Jim. This means dressing and being wheeled outside. This is part of your therapy, to get dressed with minimal assistance.

It's a real challenge. You have to become Houdini escaping the straitjacket. You have never put on socks one-handed, and putting them on a foot you can't raise or feel is a test. Your bra has hooks, which are impossible for you to do yourself, so the aide helps. Then the shirt goes over your head with your dead arm threaded through the sleeve. Your legs are threaded into loose pants.

Now Jim takes over from the aide. He wraps a scarf around your head turban style, and the aide wheels you out the door and into the elevator, and you and Jim go outside for your "walk."

But there's really no walking involved. You go outside to sit by the water and watch the ducks. Jim rests his hands on your shoulders. Tears are flowing down your cheeks. Your makeup is probably ruined now. Doesn't matter.

Jim doesn't say anything, you don't say anything, but the not saying anything says something. Something about being in the wheelchair staring at the innocent ducks with the hospital building looming over you both. The water reflects the ducks, two sets of them, up and down, ducks that didn't do a damned thing to anyone. You wonder what the hell you are doing in this dream. You wonder when someone is going to wake you.

Let Me Give You a Hand

YOU CAN'T STOP TALKING about having your nails painted.

Mom doesn't understand and asks, "Why are you so obsessed with your nails?" You realize she's looking at you from her side; her big picture didn't include fingernails. But it seems perfectly logical to you.

"It's the only thing I have control over right now," you explain. "I'm constantly staring at this lifeless hand, so it may as well look nice. I'll take the bubble gum pink polish please."

James locates a nail salon close to the rehab hospital. They don't offer services outside the salon, but Jim insists and money talks. Once Jim agrees to pay the highway robbery fee, it's scheduled.

You: an impaired body, paralyzed left side with a face that sags, making it difficult to form clear words.

The manicurist: a young Vietnamese girl who can't speak a word of English. She timidly enters the room with her tiny suitcase of manicure tools and a small foot tub.

She looks terrified.

Ever so mindful of your recovery goals, you pick a bright red nail polish, thinking the bright shade will help you keep track of your left hand. She starts painting the left hand first, but it won't lie flat. The fingers curl and become gnarly and clawlike. Every time she tries to paint, the evil hand curls and she lets fly a torrent of Vietnamese words. If she tries forcing the hand flat, it slides off the table and dangles on the side of the wheelchair.

She has on a yellow T-shirt. When she finishes the nails, it looks like she was the loser in a bloody battle.

Once the polish is applied, you stand up. Mom is lying on the bed reading a magazine. She looks up, astonished, and says, "What are you doing?"

She means, "Why are you standing up? You can't do that."

You thought you would just get up and walk over to the fan to dry the polish. So you did. Suddenly brought back to reality, you fall back into the wheelchair and slump over the young Vietnamese girl. Mom struggles with her to get you into a sitting position while at the same time wrestling with the unstable wheelchair.

Pretty weird mind games. To think you can stand and then do it—but once you're reminded of your paralysis, to collapse.

The Vietnamese manicurist has had enough. She gathers her beauty supplies and bolts from the room, leaving her jacket and a few other items. Mom has to chase after her to give her the things she's left behind.

partTWO

Judge Judy Gets Hammered

YOUR DECISION TO REFUSE more chemotherapy treatment in the rehab hospital made Dr. Jerk madder than a hornet on the inside of a window. He sent his friend and associate Dr. Panic in to see you, in an attempt to convince you.

Dr. Panic is hovering over your bed now clutching a large manila envelope.

"Hi, I'm Dr. Panic. Dr. Jerk asked me to review these CAT scans and angiograms. I haven't yet, but what you have is incurable. You may die from this disease if it goes untreated."

You're caught off guard. You had been relaxing, watching Judge Judy with your mother after a long day of therapies. Judge Judy has become your secret addiction in the rehab hospital. She puts everyone in his place. Before this conversation, you had decided that you wanted to become Judge Judy. Setting the rules and enforcing them.

Now you have to put Judge Judy in the background. Someone in a white coat, with authority, is saying you will die if you don't do as he says.

Die.

The word has black tentacles. You burst into tears.

Dr. Panic leaves and sends for the on-staff neurologist. She steps into your room and asks how you're feeling.

In between sobs, you say, "How am I supposed to feel? He just told me I'm going to die. I know we're all going to die, it's inevitable, but I'm not ready. I still have so many things to do. I need to raise my little boy. The way everyone keeps talking, I feel like I can't even cry, because I'm afraid my head may explode."

She stares at you intently but says nothing to comfort you. Her only response is to shrug her shoulders. She vanishes as suddenly as she appeared.

The phone is ringing. You are crying hard. Mom has witnessed the whole exchange and is fighting back tears, too. She answers the phone and hands it to you.

"It's your brother. John wants to talk with you."

"Hi, Johnny, I'm a little upset, I've just been told I'm going to die." You say it all between sobs.

"Okay, listen to me, Julia." John tends to get animated when he's trying to convince you. That's why he makes a great trial lawyer.

"You're upset, but LISTEN TO ME, I'M COMING OVER THERE RIGHT NOW TO UN-UPSET YOU. I'LL BE RIGHT THERE!" he screams into the phone to get his point across. You can tell he's mad—or is that fear in his voice?

You hang up the phone and continue crying with Mom. "I feel like I can't blow my nose too hard, or cry, or laugh. Any strain and my head is liable to go."

John must have used some kind of superhero method to arrive as quickly as he does. He is pacing by your bed.

"YOU ARE NOT GOING TO DIE," he continues, as though he had never put down the phone. "We're going to find out what happened and how to get well. You're not going anywhere but home to recover. You're a fighter, Julia. You're going to beat this. You're tough. Do you hear me? You are *not* going to die. How did that asshole doctor come to his conclusion?"

"He said he consulted with Dr. Jerk. The surprising thing is, he has not reviewed my films."

"Obviously, these are not the right doctors to listen to. Stick with Dr. Neuro—he hasn't said you're going to die."

"Yeah, but he hasn't exactly said I'm going to live, either. Nobody will say I'm going to live."

"But you feel secure with Dr. Neuro, right?"

"Yes."

"Then why don't you call him, for Christ's sake?"

Johnny always has a way of calming you down. Even when he's hollering at you.

YOU CALL DR. NEURO, right then and there. By the end of the call things are not quite so black and white. You're in one piece again, you're so grateful to Johnny that you make him give you a long hug, and you're wondering whether you should have given a Judge Judy response during that encounter with Dr. Panic. You imagine you're in her chair peering down at this nobody doctor: "Well, I don't believe you. Case closed. You're dismissed."

You Can Keep the Dime

THERE IS AN UNSPOKEN RULE you are learning: Nurses never answer call lights. Pushing the button by your bed will never produce a nurse, only a nurse's aide. The aides are responsible for initial contact.

You have been waiting for over fifty minutes to urinate. You can't do it yourself; you need to be helped. And you have a bladder infection. And no one is materializing. Must be the aide's lunch hour.

You keep pushing the call button, but no one responds.

What's the worst that could happen? You pee in the bed and soak everything. But what if you were choking on something? What if you fell? What if the volcano in your head went off again?

You pick up the phone and call the main switchboard from the outside line.

"How may I direct your call?" an official-sounding voice queries.

"Hi, I'm sorry to bother you but no one is answering the call button on my floor."

"Is this a joke?"

Like you're in the middle of some juvenile telephone prank. ("Is your refrigerator running? You'd better go catch it.")

"If so," the voice continues, scolding you, "it's not a very good joke. This is a hospital, and pranks like this can have serious consequences."

"My name is Julia Garrison, I'm in room 417. Please look it up. I have to be lifted to the potty chair and I've been waiting a really long time. It hurts." You sound panicked; you're extremely eager for her to take you seriously.

"I'll see what I can do."

As if you were in a joking frame of mind. You're not.

If you'd been willing to joke, you'd have said, "Ahhh, relief. Never mind. Could you send someone from housekeeping?"

The tiny Hawaiian nurse who shows up a few minutes later with her hair in a tight bun is not so approving of your resourcefulness.

"It's against procedure for patients to call the front desk," she says as she pulls the covers back and hoists you up.

"Is it against procedure to make a patient with a bladder infection wait nearly an hour to pee?" you ask.

"Just don't call the operator again."

While you're perched over the toilet, you consider singing her the old Jim Croce song "Operator" as you relieve yourself. But she's holding you up, so you think better of it.

You sing it silently inside your head, though, and when you start cackling with laughter, she doesn't seem to understand what's so funny.

Coming to Terms
with Shoe Envy

Before your stroke. Sitting at home. When your body still worked . . .

Jim walks in the room and says he's going to watch a video. He brings you a video and asks whether you want to watch it with him. He holds up the video case and shows you the title. And you look at the case, and it has the title written in big black letters and the title of the video is . . .

The title of the video Jim asks whether you want to watch is . . .

Big black letters and you can read them and the title of the video he wants to watch with you is . . .

See a woman's face, see a woman's face, see a woman's face, who is it?

HOPE IS A POWERFUL MOTIVATOR. Hope is always what gets you to the next goal; once achieved, there's the goal after that. Anyone who tries to kill the hope in your heart is the one you have to be prepared to battle. You tell yourself to remember that.

Jim walks into your hospital room and puts a box on the bed. Inside it is a pair of sneakers. Funky Converse high-tops. No support. No room for a brace.

He says, "You are going to walk."

■ ■ ■

YOU ARE SITTING IN A WAITING ROOM in a hospital and it is afternoon and there is rain falling outside. Jim is sitting next to you holding your hand. Across the hall is another woman with dark hair and birdlike features. You are both waiting for some kind of treatment. She seems to be ahead of you in line.

She has on shoes that you think are cool, but you can tell she is wearing a brace, just as you are beneath the Velcro-sealed sneakers you're wearing. She has on shoes that look fairly normal even though a leg brace is inserted in one of the shoes. You are dealing with shoe envy because wearing this clunky brace beneath your ugly geriatric shoes has you feeling just a little nostalgic. You love buying new shoes. Now you have to wear these special shoes for old people.

So many cute shoes out there—and not a pair of working feet in sight. You can never wear stylish shoes again—it's ugly flats for the rest of your life. And you're feeling a little sorry for yourself when the birdlike woman starts weeping.

And you ask her what's wrong and she doesn't want to say at first and you ask again and she explains her operation and how it went wrong and her husband left her before the accident and how there is no one to help her care for her children. She has no network of support, no family to help care for her or her kids, and she's going to lose custody.

And then there's Jim right next to you waiting with you so you won't be lonely. And all the people in your family who keep materializing by the side of your bed and asking you what you need and how they can get it for you.

She does not even have family. You wish you could help her in some way.

The nurse comes and tells her it's her turn.

"You're going to get your kids back," you tell her as the nurse leads her away. You have no idea why you would say such a thing, or if it's true. It just comes out of you.

"No, I'm not," she says. She doesn't even look back at you.

■ ■ ■

"WHAT ARE WE WAITING FOR?"

Your walls say, "Hi, remember us?" Same walls, same window, same bed. You're not in the hall. You're back in your own room.

Jim is there in the room with you and the two of you are waiting for something. You just can't recall what it is. You're lying down in the bed, so you must be finished with whatever therapy the bird lady had. You're clearly waiting, and Jim's helping you wait for it. Whatever it is.

"Your brother Joe is bringing pizza for dinner," Jim says. "Designer pizza. You're going to love it."

"Oh."

"Are you okay? You sound funny."

You should probably tell him about this face thing. Or did you?

"Jim?"

"Yeah?"

"Did I tell you about the face thing?"

"What face thing?"

"I can't feel my face anymore. It's like I'm talking through plaster."

It does take quite a bit of effort to get the words out.

"Okay."

"Plus my head hurts like hell."

"Okay. I'll get the nurse."

"I feel different, Jim."

"Okay. I'll be right back."

He's gone.

THEY ARE STRAPPING YOU to a gurney. They are putting you in an ambulance.

"Honey, they're going to take you back to the critical care hospital. It's about thirty minutes away. You're going to go in an ambulance."

You're confused. Why are you going back there? Weren't you already in a hospital?

"No. I want Jim to drive me."

Jim above you, a familiar face amid the strangers.

"You're still an inpatient, ma'am. It's not an option."

Who the hell said that?

"What is happening to me, Jim? Am I having another stroke?"

"We're going to find out, that's why we're taking the little trip to critical care. Don't worry. Let's go."

Not Jim's voice. Sky changes, noise level drops, interior roof of the ambulance slides into place.

"I want Jim to drive me. I don't want you to drive me. I want Jim driving me."

Sound of an engine gunning to life.

"Why can't Jim just drive the ambulance then?"

Sound of gears shifting, ambulance moving backward, then pivoting, then rocketing forward. Siren goes on.

You hear yourself say: "I do not give my permission for this."

Tires screech and you are moving and the straps are holding you in place and you are being violated and your face is gone.

Before your stroke. Sitting at home. When your body still worked . . .

Jim walks in the room and he's going to watch a video. Holds up the video case and shows the title to you. Can't make out the title. Big black letters.

See a woman's face see a woman's face see a woman's face on the cover of the videocassette. Who is it?

Reflections from a Metal Cage

SIREN. Ambulance moving fast. Staring at its steel-girdered ceiling, which is now vibrating like one of those big paint-can shakers at a hardware store. Out of control.

"Is Jim still behind us?"

"Yes. I can see him."

Time collapsing. Face all gone. Head hurts even worse now. Like the first time. It occurs to you that you may die. It occurs to you that you are not really here anymore. You're suspended somehow inside the metal cage they've shoved you into, and it's hurtling with a high whine, and you can see yourself locked inside it.

Can't move.

You're suffocating.

You heard yourself say, "No."

Overpowered.

Jesus.

Violated.

BEFORE YOUR STROKE. Sitting at home. When your body still worked.

Jim walks in the room and he's going to watch a video. See a woman's face.

Jodie Foster.

Jim walks in the room and he wants to watch a video and he says, "I checked out a good video for us to watch. *The Accused,* with Jodie Foster."

And he put it on and you both sat down and you both watched.

And when they got to the scene where the men attacked her, where they held her down screaming and laid into her, your body started shuddering, you couldn't control it, faster and faster, and you were sobbing and Jim wanted to know what was wrong and you couldn't say anything.

You were hovering outside of your body. You were not really there in your living room anymore. You were somewhere else.

Dad's Question

Growing up, you always referred to yourself as "Julia-wait-till-the-wedding-night-Fox."

You were preserving yourself as the one thing you could give as a gift to the person you loved. You would be the wedding gift. Your friends thought it sounded too much like a fairy tale, but it was what you believed. You just felt you could never make love to somebody without having the love that goes along with a lifetime bond with that person.

People called you a tomboy growing up. You were always a buddy with the guys, never a girlfriend. Once your father even asked you if you were a lesbian, because he couldn't understand why you didn't date. You thought about saying, "Dad, I'm so glad you brought this up. I've been struggling with how to tell you, but I'm in love, and I want to marry Tina Turner." You spared him that joke, though, and told him the truth, which was that you were just more of a buddy-type person and that you really didn't even know how to flirt.

Ray-Bans and the
Search for Cool

You spent a lot more time in the mud with boys than trying to attract their romantic interest. Every time you tried to flirt it, was pathetic. Once, as a twenty-something, you were at the auto mechanic's picking up your car after a fender bender. You were inside the garage, inside your car, and the cute mechanic was leaning in the window to talk to you. You were chatting, smiling, and doing the best you could to be flirtatious. You reached over and got the aviator sunglasses from your handbag. You put them on trying to look cool—then you noticed something slapping against your face. There was a misshapen, flecked-with-purse-dregs, out-of-its-cartridge tampon stuck in the hinge of your glasses, hanging off your face.

That was what used to happen to you when you tried to flirt. You weren't exactly a smooth operator.

For some reason the cute mechanic never posed the date question. Maybe he was turned off by your Inspector Clouseau take on female cool.

When you went to college, you were still a virgin, and you were proud of this, because most of the girls you knew weren't virgins. You weren't "experienced," but this didn't matter to you.

During your freshman year in college you had a friend named Rick.

You knew him from the year before; you had met him while visiting friends. He was nice enough and the two of you spent time together. There was nothing sexual about it. It was a friendship: talking, hanging out, like several dozen other buddies you'd had over the years who were guys.

When you eventually went to school in Vermont, Rick was still there at another college across town. You went to a party over at one of the dorms at his college.

You had been drinking keg beer (which was pretty disgusting) and partying with Rick.

Rick volunteered to give you a ride back to your dorm, and you gladly accepted.

Getting rides across town had been a bit of a dilemma for you recently, so you were relieved to know you had a ride home.

It got late. Rick's car was at his house. You left the party together.

You walked over to the house he shared with two other boys. It wasn't far.

He invited you inside. You thought for a moment, then decided to go in. Maybe if you hadn't been drinking all night, you would have insisted that it was time for you to go home. But everything seemed fine.

The minute you stepped in, he shut the door behind you.

He started kissing you, right there in the hallway. At first, you thought it was nice. But the minute he decided you didn't seem to mind him kissing you, he stopped being Rick.

You'd hardly realized it, but it suddenly dawned on you that he had been leading you somewhere. He closed another door behind you.

You wanted to leave. But he wouldn't stop kissing you.

He started ripping off your clothes.

You didn't want to have sex with him, and you told him so. It didn't matter. He kept tearing away at clothes and underwear.

You tried to make your way to the door. He threw you onto the bed and kept tearing off things.

You said, out loud, so you'd know you had said it, "Stop, please stop. I'm a virgin."

He got on top of you, held you down, and forced his way into you.

"No, you're not," he grunted. "No, you're not."

He had you pinned down. He was strong. You were utterly defenseless. Something animalistic took him over and he was no longer Rick, but Sick Rick. The nice guy had left the room and been replaced by a maniacal stranger.

You were no longer a person, but some kind of blow-up doll without human feelings.

All the time that he was violating you, you sobbed and begged him to stop, but eventually you stopped the begging and a sense of unreality came over the room and you saw yourself pinned to the bed by a stranger and heard yourself weeping.

He grunted loudly and pulled himself out of you and dragged your head over his penis, which was now limp. You heard some voices in the room, probably his two roommates, but you couldn't see anything because of the way he had you pinned. You recall thinking that he was actually proud of this.

He held your head down on his penis for what seemed like hours and you thought you would suffocate. You came very close to vomiting from the wretched smell of urine and semen. He must have sensed this, because he pulled your head away. You looked up and around. Whoever was in the room had left.

Once it was over, you eventually stopped sobbing and lay there for a long time, numb, empty, gone.

Jesus.

Violated.

Not really there.

The sun was up.

Your voice was hoarse and raspy.

You asked as quietly as you could if he could get you home now. You didn't want to agitate him, so you asked very humbly and very submissively.

He nodded and left the room, closing the door behind him.

You realized that, if you played your cards right, you might actually get out of this alive.

You scrambled to find your clothes. Your underwear had vanished. You put on your pants and your sweater sans undergarments. Each had been torn.

You opened the door and looked out. His roommates were passed out in the front living room. You saw him jostle them awake and ask them to go with him, with the promise they'd all go to breakfast. His treat.

Rick had an older Mustang with bucket seats in the front. There were lots of fast-food cartons strewn in the car. You got in the back. The three boys sat in the front, with one of them sitting where the gearshift was located. They didn't want to even sit in the back with you. One guy offered gum to the other guys in the front. As they unwrapped the gum and popped it in their mouths, they rolled the wrappers up and took shots at you with the gum wrappers. This amused them so much that they found other discarded wrappings and threw those at you, too. They were having lots of fun and laughing at this game. They dumped you at your dormitory.

It was a weekend, and the dormitory was empty. Everyone had gone home to the safety of parents and family.

You climbed the stairs to the second floor where your room was. You walked into the shower stall fully dressed. You turned on the water as hot as it could get. Your body leaned against the flowing hot water in the stall for a long time, until the shower head ran cool.

But you were not there.

Years later, you were on the Cape with some friends at a club where young adults and college-age kids would go to get drunk and meet members of the opposite sex. You noticed a man with dark hair trying to catch your eye. He looked familiar.

When you realized it was Sick Rick, your stomach went cold.

You were speechless. You just stood there gawking. He must have mistaken your staring as a come-on, because he made his way across the bar to you. You thought surely he'd say your name or apologize or some-thing, but he didn't even recognize you now. You had lost weight and cut your long hair and were a few years older.

He said, "It's been a while since I've come across a smile as nice as yours."

Not only did he have no memory of you, he was trying to pick you up.

You stared at him for a moment. Then you threw your drink in his face.

You motioned to your friends and left the bar without looking back.

Déjà Vu

THE DRIVER SILENCES the blaring siren as the ambulance squeals to a halt at the emergency entrance. You feel like a prisoner in the metal cage of the ambulance cargo area. You hear the latch on the rear door click. Two attendants silently roll your wheeled bed through the automatic doors and into the corridor.

The lights of the ambulance continue to whir as you are rushed to an examining room.

"Why am I back here? I've already done this." Are you dreaming? You feel as though you're watching a sci-fi movie where someone keeps hitting rewind, play, rewind, play, over and over.

"I've already seen this movie." You hear a voice in the room say, "She might be hallucinating." The nurses are going about the business of taking your vital signs and talking among themselves. "She was sent from the rehab hospital. They were concerned that she might be about to stroke again. Her neurologist is Dr. Neuro. I called him at home. He wants her admitted once she is stabilized."

You're not there.

Why does the IV feel so real in this dream—sticking, poking, prodding. As usual the phlebotomist has difficulty finding a vein.

Suddenly, you realize that Jim is beside you. "Thank God you're here, Jim. I thought I was dreaming. Are we going back to the rehab hospital now? Joe brought pizza."

"You're being admitted for observation. Dr. Neuro is going to see you in the morning. Don't worry, it'll be okay."

You both wonder if that is so.

It's after two in the morning when you are moved to a room. Jim kisses you good night and heads home, still wondering. You're exhausted, but you can't sleep.

Residents Out for Blood

Edie and your mom were in a bridge club for thirty years. She made you things when you were a little girl. Clothing for your dolls. A doily for their tiny table. Edie is on your mind a lot for some reason.

"WHAT ARE ALL THESE BLOOD TESTS FOR and who ordered them?" You are staring at a little bearded nurse who is trying to smile.

A different young fellow. A new and yet-to-be-experienced level of incompetence. Your veins are virtually impossible for even seasoned professionals to locate. Yesterday your mother left during one of the blood draws, while you were talking to the guy doing it in your Dracula voice and asking if he was related to Bela Lugosi. She didn't laugh, even though he did. She simply couldn't watch it anymore. She probably slept poorly last night. You know how she is about seeing you get poked and prodded constantly.

Nurse Beard smiles harder. "Ma'am, one of the residents ordered three tests for us this afternoon, okay. So could I get you to just go ahead and hold out your arm, please?"

You glare at him.

"Actually, no, you can't have my arm, or my blood. It's time for me to ask you questions. Less than five minutes ago, had you ever set eyes on me before? No, you hadn't. Right? Right. Now. Time for another question. What the hell is the resident's authority? No answer? No answer. Third question. I've already had these three blood tests. True? Don't just stare at me, take a look at the goddamned chart. True?"

Shuffle shuffle shuffle.

"Uh . . . accurate, yes."

You have successfully split the entire neurology staff into factions. Each one has a theory. Each one has a diagnosis. Each one has an agenda. They are each pricking you like a pincushion to prove how smart they are. And they are not even reading their own notations. You have a feeling you know which one of them it was who ordered these tests, too. The brisk little brunette with her hair tied in a bun who never talks to you, only past you, never looks you in the eye. You wish she was close enough to slap.

"Please tell the resident I'm refusing any more blood tests from anyone other than my primary neurologist, Dr. Neuro. And while you're at it, tell the resident who ordered these tests that if she wants to be considered any kind of doctor, she should take thirty seconds to look at a patient's records before ordering tests. Okay. If she gives you a hard time, tell her to see the patient, me— the boss."

He leaves.

Testing Your Patient

DR. NEURO, your neurologist, visits you. The only person in a white coat who seems capable of looking you in the eye. Tall, patient, calm Dr. Neuro. You remember liking him and trusting him, which is an achievement at a time when your memory is not always totally reliable. He makes you feel safe. He has huge hands. His right hand amazes you when he extends it for you to shake.

"You missed me and wanted me back, right?" you joke. He smiles, and nods, and asks about your symptoms. You tell him everything you can think of. He writes down what you say.

He tells you Dr. Jerk's diagnosis is still very much in doubt. Dr. Neuro, of the huge hands, tells you he has arranged for some tests to try to clarify Dr. Jerk's theory. He apologizes for the number of tests they're running on you. He apologizes for not knowing everything.

He means it. You can tell.

As it turns out, vasculitis (Dr. Jerk's favorite disease) commonly presents in the lower intestinal organs. Dr. Neuro wants an ultrasound of your lower organs to look for evidence of vasculitis. If that proves negative, it will be time for another angiogram.

Then Dr. Neuro tells you he won't be at the hospital for the next week, due to an unexpected family situation. He reassures you, saying that you'll be in the care of the head of the neurology unit.

You are surprised by how nervous this piece of news makes you. You know he has put you in the best of hands while he's gone, but you feel more secure with him than with the head of neurology.

You realize you have confidence and a sense of security with Dr. Neuro. You don't want to keep repeating your medical history over and over again with new people. He assures you that the covering doctor will be informed personally about your case. He asks if you need anything. You tell him, "Yes, I need my left side back."

He smiles and squeezes your hand in his huge hand. He goes.

It's night and you're all alone. The hall outside your room is dark and empty.

Everything stops. The hospital is so quiet it frightens you. A storehouse of wounded strangers. You wonder what other lives have been altered forever by some catastrophic illness or injury. The neuro floor must have some gruesome stories.

You wish Jim were next to you. You want to lie on your side with your arms around him.

A Piece of Your Mind

IN ADDITION TO THE GAMUT of tests that awaited you when you returned to the critical care hospital, they are asking you to consider approving a brain biopsy. The neurology staff is recommending this procedure to determine if you truly have cerebral vasculitis.

Since you refused another chemotherapy treatment at the rehab hospital, Dr. Doogie, your radiologist, has taken a personal interest in you. He's come to visit you on his days off to help you sort out the medical questions. One of those questions is pretty basic.

"What," you asked, "is a brain biopsy?"

"It's when a burrow hole is drilled into a quiet area of the brain, and sample brain tissue is removed."

Okay . . .

"What," you continue, "is a quiet area? There's nothing quiet about me—unless maybe you count the whole right side of my brain, which I guess is now considered dead."

"A quiet area is a spot in the brain that would not affect any functions. It's usually behind the ear."

"See," you explain to Dr. Doogie, "I'm thinking I need to keep whatever I have left, quiet or not."

"You want conclusive evidence about whether you're suffering from this incurable disease, right?"

"Right."

"Brain biopsy is the way to go."

"The only way to rule this out?"

"Yes."

The possibility of certainty is very appealing to you.

"Okay. Then poke as many holes as you need to. I just want a goddamn diagnosis."

You have been poked, prodded, and tested for so long in a hospital environment that you just want a straight answer. You just want to get it over with.

BUT JIM CONSULTS with his doctor brother-in-law, Pete, who tells him that a brain biopsy is an invasive procedure that could cause all kinds of complications. When he hears this, Jim is against doing it. He feels that if the test isn't going to be conclusive, it isn't worth the risk.

Dr. Doogie then comes back to explain that the results could come back negative, but that you still might have the disease in a different area than the one that was sampled.

"So will they poke holes all over my head like a colander to keep checking until they find something?"

"No, there would only be one biopsy at a time."

"What would you do if it were you?"

"I don't know. It's a tough decision. Cerebral vasculitis is extremely rare and it's already been determined there's no evidence of the disease in your lower organs."

Dr. Jerk saunters into the room while you are discussing the biopsy with Dr. Doogie. You can tell he's miffed that you're even considering it.

Dr. Jerk has made the preliminary diagnosis of possible vasculitis, but without a brain biopsy showing the diseased cells, he is "working on an assumption." He insists that you be treated with the standard drugs used for vasculitis.

He is not pleased that you have refused the second chemotherapy treatment while in the rehab hospital. You are still arguing that you don't want to push it: Additional chemotherapy seems like an extreme step, and a great way to make absolutely sure you become sterile.

You want to have another child.

He brushes this off—again. "At least you have Rory." As if to say: Isn't that enough for you? "I have an only child," he continues, "and it's great."

"Well," you counter, "that's your choice, not mine, and I don't want science changing my options."

"Don't you think it would have been wise to consult me about the brain biopsy?" Dr. Jerk asks. "All the other doctors are still testing and diagnosing you. I'm actually treating you."

Sensing a fight in the offing, Dr. Doogie leaves the room.

"That's why I didn't consult you," you tell him, looking him straight in the eye. "You've already made up your mind about what I have. I don't believe your diagnosis is correct, and Dr. Neuro is not so sure either. At least he knows enough to say when he doesn't know something. What if the biopsy proved negative? Then what would your treatment be for me?"

"It would be the same either way—chemotherapy monthly for life. That is the correct treatment for your disease."

Talk about not letting the facts get in the way of your work.

"Look," you say, "I want to be absolutely sure I've got this disease you say I have before I poison my body for the rest of my life. My gut is telling me I don't have this. I trust my gut, which is my consciousness, which is ultimately my soul. You've heard of a soul, right? I mean, did you, you know, get one during orientation?"

"The only way to get a conclusive diagnosis is through your autopsy," Dr. Jerk snarls.

You're stunned. "Well, I'm not going to rush to have that procedure."

Dr. Jerk snorts, and then bolts out of the room in a huff.

Your relationship with him, now openly contentious, has been deteriorating for so long that it is, you can tell, at odds with your becoming healthy. He is so bent on being right that he simply can't see anything but his own opinion.

A FEW MINUTES LATER Dr. Jerk is standing at your bedside.

"I've set up an appointment with Dr. Guru in Ohio. He's the premier expert on vasculitis disease. He actually is doing me a favor by seeing you. I've already consulted him. You will fly to Ohio to have him examine you. Of course, he deserves to get paid for his time."

"When did you make this appointment for?"

"When you're released from the hospital in a few weeks. You should feel privileged to see him. He's going to confirm my diagnosis." Dr. Jerk was giddy with pride that he had such a powerful connection.

"Wait a minute. I'm supposed to fly to his hospital, have Jim take time off and leave my three-year-old, and go halfway across the country to talk to a guy who you already know is going to confirm your diagnosis? I don't call that opinion, I call that collusion. I'm not doing it. Anyway, I've already decided I'm not going to do the brain biopsy. Jim doesn't want me to; it's too inconclusive."

"You're making a mistake by not seeing Dr. Guru. He doesn't consent to see just anybody."

"Well, I don't consent to see him. It's too bad he won't get the pleasure of meeting me."

"You're being an obstinate fool. I'm trying to help you."

"Obstinate. That's a new label for me, I already have denial and impulsive. I prefer determined, positive, and hopeful. I've got news for you: I want to have another baby, and I'll be Rollerblading with Rory before too long."

"Make no mistake, my dear. You really are in DENIAL." He turns on his heel and leaves.

Just as the door starts to close, you holler, "MAKE NO MISTAKE. I'M NOT YOUR DEAR."

Return to Sender

THE CRITICAL CARE DOCTORS establish that you did not have another stroke. You realize that the shooting pains that occur intermittently in your head do not necessarily foretell another stroke. Although the medical staff doesn't say so, you conclude that you had a panic attack when you were at the rehab hospital. You come to learn that these attacks will plague you. You devise methods to calm yourself when the attacks occur. Breathe. Breathe. Go somewhere pleasant. Snatch a good memory, relive it. Narrow River.

Five days have passed since you were readmitted to the critical care hospital. It's time to resume rehabilitation. The thought of leaving this safe haven to return to the dismal rehab institution depresses you. Not only is the critical care staff attentive, but the food here is so much better.

The first time you were sent to the rehab hospital you were excited to be moving on, taking the next step in your recovery. You didn't know what to expect. Now you know what's ahead of you, and you wish you could skip Go and head for home.

The ambulance attendants hoist you on the bed with wheels,

strap you in, and take you on another expensive taxi ride. This isn't the ride of your life, but the ride *for* your life, as you are yet again ferried from one hospital to another.

They bring you back to the neurology floor. This time you don't joke with the attendants that they've taken you to the wrong place. You remain quiet. What has happened to your life?

YOU ARE ANNOYED at your own body generally, and at your head specifically.

You like wearing the cool headdresses that people keep bringing you. One aide from Haiti has a talent for doing your headdress, and when she's working, she sings Haitian songs to you. You like it when she shows up. It makes you feel like another person, which in your current situation is a good thing.

ONE DAY YOU ARE SITTING in bed feeling good, having just been sung to and having just had the scar on your head concealed by an intricate Haitian-wrapped headdress, when a tall woman walks into your room, looks down at you in the bed, and says, "Are you Julia Fox from Andover?"

Stunned, you say, "Yes." She does look familiar.

"I'm Misty Mouse. I went to high school with you."

Her face is reassembling itself for you into something familiar— but with two decades layered on top.

Misty. This is weird.

"What are you doing here, Misty?"

Maybe they're planning some kind of reunion meant to keep your spirits up? What is going on?

"I work here. I'm a physical therapist. I'll be by to check in on you now and then, okay?"

Misty. Yes. You went to high school together. Math class. Miss Corcoran. But you were in a class of five hundred kids.

"You recognized me?"

"Sure."

Gentle eyes. Helped you with math homework. She was very popular.

"Did I look this bad in high school, that you could recognize me twenty years later?"

THE FOURTH FLOOR is the neurology floor and there are a lot of brain issues. One particular woman wails and screams constantly. You are fortunate to have a single room so you don't have to share anyone else's misery. Your door can shut. Even with your door closed, though, you can hear The Wailer. Two in the morning, ten in the morning, four in the afternoon. Doesn't matter. The Wailer howls and bellows.

One day you ask a nurse, "Does that woman have a roommate?" Yes, she does. You can't imagine how the roommate handles it.

Then you ask, "The lady who's screaming right now, is she aware of what she is doing?" Yes, she is. The nurse explains that she just can't communicate with words anymore. But yes, she knows what she's doing.

She knows what she's doing. She does it anyway.

It surprises you that this fact makes you as angry as it does. But she is affecting everybody on the floor, and she is choosing to howl like that. The Wailer is driving her roommate, and you, and everyone else on the floor absolutely mad. And she is doing it on purpose.

She howls out again, and breaks into little sobs.

"What a bitch," you hear yourself say.

Pardon Me, but You're Incompetent

YOU ARE IN A HOSPITAL BED. Again. The halls are empty and quiet. Must be a weekend or late at night. Or both.

A young male Asian nurse is by your side, attempting to draw blood. You can't believe the pain; he's missing the vein, he's using a heavy-gauge needle, and he's obviously inexperienced with difficult veins, which, you have learned in recent months, you have. He seems to imagine that you are a bolt of fabric being pinned into clothing.

"What time is it?" you ask. There's no window in this room.

"A little after two in the morning," he says.

"Is there another nurse on call?"

He looks up from your arm and stares at you.

"Why?"

"Just tell me whether there's another nurse available, okay?"

Silence.

"I guess so."

You look him in the eye. "You have to stop. I'm sorry, but I need you to get the most experienced phlebotomist you can. You're not having much success with this blood draw, and you're really hurting me."

You don't know why you feel you have to apologize for his ineptitude, but it seems to make your request a little nicer.

A Lot of Fuktion

JIM IS CONCERNED about your separation from Rory. He goes to great lengths to make sure Rory sees you regularly. He makes attempts to keep it light for Rory by bringing in books for you to read to him in your bed.

"Look, Mommy, I brought you Elmo to keep you company so you won't be lonely," Rory exclaims excitedly as he enters your room. "He has a boo-boo on his head too and he needs to stay in the hospital with you until you both get better."

You eye Elmo's red, furry, limp body. There's a Band-Aid on his head. It makes your eyes well up, and you smile at the same time.

"Well, we're both going to get better real soon. What book did you bring for me to read to you?"

He hands you *Bob the Builder* and Jim props him up next to you in bed. You have difficulty balancing the book with one hand, and you can't turn the pages.

"Rory, can you help read the book with me and turn the pages?"

"I don't want to read my books here," he says. "I want you to read them to me at home."

You glance at Jim, whose face is stony and sad.

"Right now," you say, "we get to read stories in this special bed together—but only for a little while. Look at this magical bed, the buttons make it go up and down." You show him the buttons and his attention is diverted to pushing the head up and the feet down. He's thrilled with the buttons, and delights in the ride he's giving you.

MOM TELLS YOU that Rory has made a habit of asking which hospital he'll be going to today, and it makes you feel helpless and sad. On one visit Rory notices all the construction activity happening around the hospital, shakes his head, and matter-of-factly states, "There's sure lots of fuktion going on around here."

It seems accurate enough.

BACK WHEN YOU WERE WORKING FULL-TIME, you felt guilty shuffling him off to your friend Berbie's or your mom's. You'd have a Friday-night date night where you and he would have a burger in the food court and then go for a ride on the merry-go-round in the pavilion. Now you have a completely different set of guilty feelings. Back then, you could have changed the workaholic behavior, but you didn't. Now there seems to be nothing at all you can do to improve the time you spend with him.

Honey

WHAT IS THAT thing behind the wall? That thing is beautiful, but what does it do, and how does it make the wall shudder that way?

Window shut. Night dark. The ward is quiet, humming at you softly. The wall vibrates and breathes in and out and wisps into a fog and then behind it are two eyes.

Oh, right. They gave you something for sleeping.

The wall is completely gone.

Edie is looking at you, but it's hard to say when or why or where you are, how old either of you are. She must be older than you, but it's hard to tell now, looking at her. Just Edie's eyes, that's all you see.

You remember when Edie told you, "It will be okay, honey," when she picked you up from the playground when you fell as a little girl and your knee was suddenly shiny with blood and you cried out.

You remember liking when Edie said "honey." She said it to you a lot.

You remember when Edie said, "I call you honey because I love you."

It Ain't Spring Showers

YOU GET FRIENDLY with all the aides at rehab and start lobbying them to put you first on the shower list.

There is a good reason for this politicking. If you are not one of the first few to be showered, there is inevitably a huge backup; sometimes the shower wheelchair is in use and when your turn comes you have to use a potty chair. The shower chair is better than the rolling toilet chair because it has hooks to hold your shower stuff and it doesn't look as degrading as you're wheeled down the hall.

Being wheeled around in a toilet chair in a worn-out hospital johnny draped like a shawl around you is your current nominee for Indignity Number One. The whole arrangement leaves you completely exposed to any curious hallway passerby. You know you truly look brain damaged. You look like Jack Nicholson in *One Flew Over the Cuckoo's Nest* after he receives shock treatment and is faking being deranged. But your look is the real thing.

You have learned to stare down anyone who gazes at you, but you'd rather take the first shower and avoid the spectacle of being rolled around half naked with a bucket of toiletries on your lap.

■　■　■

THE SHOWER ROUTINE itself is humiliating. You are rolled to a dank shower room. It is the size of a large walk-in closet, with a shower-head on either side of the doorway. It is dim with mildew green tile, and it is cluttered with other people's handicap equipment. (You have no idea how the stuff ended up being left there. Did someone need it coming in, but not going out?)

In this room, you're hosed down in your chair like a car at a carwash. It's a depressing experience. You feel like a prisoner in your own body, like the prisoners you can see caged in the jail across the street from the hospital.

Brushing your teeth in the shower room always causes frustration. Inevitably, either you or the aide drops the toothbrush, and as you stare once again at your toothbrush, which is lying on the floor of the filthiest shower floor it has ever been your duty to scan, you always feel like screaming.

The aide picks it up and puts it on your lap. Like you would ever use it again. Only if you were brain damaged beyond reason. Which you are not. Frustrated, yes. Confused, yes. Grossed out, yes. But not that brain-damaged.

You beg your folks to bring you a fresh supply of tooth-brushes.

Eventually you have your mom tie an idiot string that connects your wrist to the toothbrush. Problem solved.

THIS MORNING, you are in the shower chair, and are being wheeled to the morning shower by a nurse who is new to the job. You need to have a bowel movement as you are being wheeled to the shower room. It's an opportunity that you can't afford to miss since you have had a history of constipation.

The nurse lifts you onto the toilet located directly across from the shower room. She leaves the room door wide open, however, and neglects to pull the curtain shut, leaving you completely exposed. Hospital staff, patients, and visitors are passing by in the corridor, getting an unsolicited peep show.

You say, "Please shut the door. I'm not an animal in the zoo."
She does.

"This really sucks, but I can't wipe myself. Could you please help me? Maybe if you pretend I'm your daughter, you'll think of me as a human being."

You can't wait to get home full-time.

You Have to Be Dead to
Get That Arrangement

YOUR FRIEND PAUL'S HUMOR leans to the macabre. He contacted several florists requesting that they send you a cross made with flowers—the kind of arrangement that people lay at a graveside or deliver to a funeral parlor. None of the florists would go for it because the person he wanted the flowers delivered to was the same person whose name he wanted on the cross.

He tells you about this during a visit, and you both laugh hysterically. You're kind of glad he didn't manage to do it, though, because it wouldn't do your family members much good to walk into your room and see a huge funeral display. But when you think of him trying earnestly to convince a florist to send a funeral arrangement to someone who's still very much alive, you feel very, very grateful to Paul for his ability to laugh at the dark side of things.

This, you realize, is the kind of stuff that will keep you going. After all, what is the alternative? To hold court in the hospital with all your friends and relatives in a state of unrelenting gloom? To bring everyone down with you? Where would that lead? Eventually people would only visit out of obligation, or stop coming altogether.

"My goal," you tell Paul, "is to be that person you'd cross the street to see, rather than the person you'd cross the street to avoid."

Where You Aren't

You remember when Edie made the bedding for your son Rory's crib.

Edie has very honest eyes. She is looking at you right now and you are looking back and her eyes say, "You're not in a hospital," but they don't need words to say it.

You say, "I'm not?"

Her open eyes say, "No. I'm in a hospital, you're coming to visit me."

And all that matters is that Edie made the bumper pad, the rocking chair, all the components that pull the pieces together in your son Rory's nursery, and her eyes could never, ever tell you a lie.

Edie makes her eyes say, "Don't worry, honey," and dim themselves, and the wall settles in again.

The Moaning Lady

You start asking questions about the lady who keeps howling at all hours of the day, even though she knows she's driving everybody nuts.

The nurses tell you the woman is in her early forties. She has had a severe left-hemisphere stroke that caused aphasia, a major brain dysfunction that damages speech and the ability to express thought.

She used to be a schoolteacher.

She had married for the first time in the past year.

Her husband is a big strapping guy who is completely devoted to her. He visits all the time.

Her stay in the hospital has already been a long one. She has been there for four months.

You ask when she's likely to get out.

"She's indefinite," the nurse tells you.

It stops you cold. Parts of you are paralyzed and you have a lot of body-part issues and some cognitive problems. But at least you are able to talk and communicate with others. This woman is trapped inside her head without the ability to express herself. Your prison is a portion of the hospital—hers is her skull, and she has no idea when or if she is getting out.

It occurs to you that there must be a lot of people like this in a lot of hospitals, people who have a worse struggle than you do.

PAUL'S VISIT IS OVER. You're on your own again. He left some cologne for you. You spray a little of it on your wrist, and then in the air, watch the droplets scatter and disperse into the air, close your eyes, and take a deep breath.

Heaven.

Disabled Chariot

FOR MOST PEOPLE a wheelchair conjures up ideas like illness, debilitation, and helplessness. It's hard to escape these preconceptions when you find yourself spending time in one.

You find that when you're sitting in a wheelchair your personality changes because you're not at the same level physically as everyone else. You're actually at the level of everyone's crotch and people have to talk down to you. "Talking down" to a person is slang for talking negatively.

Your wheelchair offers a very uncomfortable seat, no matter how you rig it. Extra cushions and pillows work only for a few minutes. After a stroke that causes paralysis, one side of the body doesn't shift. As a result, your body doesn't shift and you're constantly putting weight on one side. Shifting your body is a natural response, but with a stroke, it has to be a conscious thought. After a while the cushions don't do the trick.

WHY IS IT that when you're sitting in a wheelchair, people think you're deaf?

People treat you differently when you're in a wheelchair. In a store, salespeople are standing and you're being talked down to. Sometimes they don't even acknowledge you and speak to the person pushing you, as if you're not there. You think they figure you're powerless, that you can't even get around on your own strength. So it's best to talk to the one who got you there on two feet, the one who is steering you.

Or do they act that way because they're fearful, because they don't want to acknowledge the possibility that human beings suffer physical trauma?

No one ever teaches etiquette on how to deal with someone who's not able bodied. Maybe they figure your body is fragile, so your emotions must be as well. Or maybe they feel they simply can't risk hurting your feelings. Not out of any consideration for you, but because it would be too uncomfortable for them.

You decide that most people who don't acknowledge you must do so because they're protecting themselves, because they simply can't cope with your illness. Illness makes some people feel too vulnerable to their own emotions.

This kind of person typically comments, "God knew you had the strength to handle it." You think, "Huh? What the hell does that mean?" You begin translating this idiotic comment as "Thank God it was you and not me!"

You're tempted to ask, "Since you know God's thoughts so well, what else is he telling you?"

WHEELCHAIRS ARE EXTREMELY CUMBERSOME for something that's meant to help human beings be more mobile. You quickly realize that if you need to get somewhere first by car, and then get mobile on the street, it can actually cause injury to package the chair and load it into the car.

Some towns are definitely handicap unfriendly, something you didn't notice until you had attached a chair with wheels to your ass.

The wheelchair, you are told repeatedly, has brakes on the wheels to keep it from rolling. Mastering the brakes is the first step to master when using the chair. The therapists drill in the "safety first" mantra incessantly.

■ ■ ■

YOU WANT TO BECOME more independent. You think, "I should at least be able to brush my teeth at the sink. I'll use the wheelchair." Jim usually brushes your teeth in bed before leaving the hospital for the night.

One morning you decide you are going to get to the sink at the foot of your bed to brush your teeth. You maneuver the wheelchair and work your way to the sink only a few feet away. It's a difficult feat considering you have only one hand to push the wheel. Initially it appears that you're going to spin in circles like that crazy teacup ride at the amusement park, but then you figure it out. Proud of your accomplishment, you struggle to stand at the sink. Wobbly, but determined, you get up. You have an ever so brief moment of satisfaction when you see, out of the corner of your eye, the wheelchair roll away from you.

Oops. Forgot to lock the wheels.

Now the wheelchair is six feet away and you're clinging to the sink for dear life with your only useful hand. You're not even near the call button. You are not in the sight line of the open door. You might as well be stranded on a deserted island.

You have to wait to be discovered. After what seems like a month, a nurse breezes in.

She scolds you for impulsive behavior. She reminds you of how dangerous it is not asking for assistance. She tells you you're impulsive for not locking your wheelchair.

Okay. If you've been in a wheelchair all of your life and you've already formed habits like locking your wheelchair, then failing to do so might be considered impulsive and dangerous. But when you're being introduced to this new way of life, you don't think of these things. More fucking labeling. Suddenly your condition required you to be in a wheelchair. It didn't mean that you automatically knew how to function in that wheelchair. It doesn't just happen instantly. It feels unnatural.

"Nurse, do you ever get the urge to slap someone? I do. That would be truly impulsive of me, if I acted on that urge. So you should be thankful I'm not impulsive."

ONE SUNDAY AFTERNOON Jim wheels you outside for a stroll toward North Station. You're several blocks away from the hospital when suddenly the wheelchair spits out the front right wheel. After a few feeble attempts to do surgery by reattaching the wheel, you suggest that he leave you curbside and return with a working chair. "Give me a tin cup and maybe I could make some money while waiting. I can probably make a lot of money; I'm so pitiful looking! I can hold a cardboard sign—Need Money for New Wheels."

Jim ignores you; with all his might, he pops a wheelie, putting your weight on the hind wheels of the chair. It's like a wheelbarrow but in reverse. He has to negotiate curbs, potholes, and general street debris. He is holding the handlebars down so that your feet are up in the air. You're looking up at him. "You're my hero."

It must have been an odd scene for the passersby: Maybe a pair of homeless people had just discovered a wheelchair and were taking it back to their campsite.

Jim is sweating profusely by the time you arrive at the hospital. No wonder—you're no waif, and you're dead weight, too. He's breathing heavily and he looks like he's on the verge of collapse. You feel like screaming, "Get this man on a gurney—stat!"

SOMETIMES YOU FALL while trying to sit up by yourself in a chair.

Sometimes you fall while trying to get out of bed.

Sometimes you fall when you are practicing walking.

You fall when loved ones are there in the rehab hospital visiting you.

You fall when there is no one in the room to notice you have fallen.

Sometimes you fall in your dreams.

The key to falling and surviving, you eventually learn, is relaxing whatever can still be relaxed before you hit the floor.

Falling is a side effect of your injury. It is a fact. You must accept that it happens. It is now part of who you are. This is sometimes difficult for your loved ones to accept. At first, Jim would get frustrated and upset when you were lying on the floor. Now he gets so sad when he sees you fall. He doesn't say anything, but you can see him collapsing inside when you look up from the floor. He tells you he hates to see you on the floor and wants to save you from hurting yourself. He's in more pain than you are when it happens.

This morning you stop him as he is coming to help the therapist pick you up for what must have been the tenth time within an hour and a half.

"Jim," you say, "if I'm not falling, I'm not making any progress. I've got to learn it all over again, and I have to fall if I'm going to learn anything. Do you understand? I have to keep trying to move forward. And sometimes that means I have to fall backward. Okay? I'm going to mend, don't worry."

You know that's the same kind of response as "Be careful." It doesn't change anything. What else can you say, you wonder.

"And, guess what," you say. "I think I'm starting to bounce!"

He nods. You let him pick you up.

"Honey," you say, "I keep falling for you over and over again. You're my prince!"

You start again.

Fall Down Seven Times,
Get Up Eight

Moving your way up a ladder. Step by step.

IMPACT. The smell of alcohol and people and linoleum. Face cold against the floor. More walking practice with the therapist.

Your mom is watching.

"Oh, honey, be careful."

She constantly tells you to "be careful." As though the words will prevent you from falling, as though the falling is because you're careless. She says it because she's deeply concerned for you, but she doesn't realize that when you fall, it is not because you are being careless or failing to put safety as a high enough priority in your mind. You're *being* careful. You're falling anyway.

Parts of your body that look like they are connected to you are following their own rules, or vanishing completely without any warning. That's the problem.

It's true, though, that you've never been a particularly cautious person, and it is difficult to get into the overcautious frame of mind necessary to move your body from point A to point B. So you say, "Okay," when she says, "Be careful."

■ ■ ■

STAIRS ARE THE number one enemy. Overactive muscle tone makes your knee impossible to bend. You never can tell when it's going to happen, but it happens a lot when you're trying to make it down a flight of stairs. Today, as your mother watches, your knee locks, and the spasms travel up your leg to the hip, locking it in place. Your leg has just become a stilt. The stairs and the landing zoom into a close-up. The therapist grabs your belt at the last moment, preventing another full-force head impact, which is nice, but you are flat on your face again.

"Be careful."

The Quasimodo Walk

YOU CAN ONLY DO A FEW STEPS, with the aid of two people, before you are tired and too unsteady to continue. And it's not so much walking as assisted striding.

You require three aides to get you "walking" again. One is holding your knee to prevent it from inverting to hyperextension. Another is holding your waist to keep you upright. And a third is leading you while rolling a full-length mirror on wheels with his feet.

Your left knee keeps violently hyperextending—you can see in the mirror that it looks inside out. It snaps backward so hard you can hear bones and tendons cracking. Although you have a disconnect with your limb, you know you're causing damage. All the therapists' faces contort when they hear this snapping sound, which is pretty frequent.

"I didn't realize having a stroke could make me double-jointed. Such benefits I'm going to have. Once I get this walking thing down, I'm going to try out for the Boston Ballet."

OVER A WEEK of having three pairs of hands stabilize you pays off. Eventually, you're able to stand on your own. This achievement allows you to go to "brace clinic," where you can get an assessment for future mobility. Aides place you between parallel bars with a spotter in front and a spotter behind. You hold one bar with your right hand.

You feel as though you're in a high school gymnastic event, with the doctor as the judge. The trophy awarded would be the right to hear the words "You'll walk again." An award you had, but lost. An award you've taken for granted since you were fifteen months old.

You psych yourself to walk.

Your sheer determination grants you two very clumsy steps. But they are enough to prove wrong the people who were telling you that you'd never walk again.

When the doctor who's watching you says, "You'll walk again," you feel great. You already knew that, but it's a reward to hear it.

He won't say when, though.

"Okay," you ask. "Where's the test for my left hand. Do you have a knitting circle here? You know, I used to play the piano—are my recital days over? How about a sing-along for all the neuro patients?"

THE FACT IS, it's very hard to walk when you can't quite identify where your body is. You stare at the feet and order them to move in harmony, but it is as if your brain is a radio tuner trying, and failing, to get a lock on a clear station.

It's not that your left side is unresponsive. It's that it's missing. If you don't have any weight on your leg, you don't know where your leg is.

"I think she's had enough."

Talking about you as though you're not there again, but you're too tired to protest. They wheel you back to your room.

"Did you see that stairwell at the end of the hall there?"

A fading nurse with no discernable facial features is pouring you back into bed; she nods indulgently.

"I'm going to make it up that thing."

The nurse is now the color of dusk, a vague outline.

Her voice: "Sure you are, dear."

ONCE YOU'RE ABLE to walk ten feet, you ask the therapist to work with you on the stairwell. Thank God for the alertness of this therapist; you come close to falling over the railing and down a flight of stairs. She grips you by the waist of your pants, giving you a wedgie up to your throat—but keeping you from hurtling downward, which is something you're getting a lot of experience at. You think you may have to have surgery to remove your wedgie, though.

When you walk now, you want to do it reciprocally—right foot, then left foot. Supposedly, you're not ready for this. But you make her make you do it. And you do.

THE PLAN IS TO VISIT your house again, then ride to your folks' house thirty minutes away to visit your family and your son, Rory. The doctors think it will be good for your outlook. Jim has had to get several lessons from the physical therapists on transferring you in and out of a car, no mean feat. He also talks about the time you both spent learning how to get you in and out of the house without a wheelchair ramp.

Either these events took place without you or your memory is collapsing again.

As he drives you home, you stare out the window and are in awe of everything. It has been, you are told, two months since your stroke.

The landscape looks different and the same. The colors are intense. You feel as though you are seeing things for both the first and the last time. It's as though you've been blind since birth and have miraculously recovered the gift of sight.

You arrive home, and Jim backs the car into the garage. You sit staring at the cul-de-sac, the neighbors' houses, and your yard. He wrestles the wheelchair, and you, into the house.

You're back.

You left here a hundred years or so ago as Julia, a working mom. You don't know what you are now. You're broken.

If you cry, Jim will cry, too. So you don't. But everything is on the brink of death in the house: the plants, your neglected and apparently underfed cat Winnie, and you. Jim has been working, taking care of Rory, driving to and from your folks' place, and visiting you in the hospital.

Jim asks if you need anything. It occurs to you that you would love to lie down on your own bed. You ask Jim if he can get you upstairs.

He wheels the chair to the stairs. He maneuvers you to a sitting position on the steps, then drops down and scoops you up, almost, as a fireman would. But he doesn't really "carry" you up the stairs—it's half carrying, and half dragging.

"Honey," you say, "it's like the scene in *Gone With the Wind*. You're Rhett, I'm Scarlett."

He flops you on the bed. You lie together in silence, both sweating profusely from the workout.

"I'm going to make it up that thing," you tell him, before you doze off.

"I know you are," he answers.

Musical Chairs

YOU LEAVE YOUR HOME and set off for your parents' house, where the whole family has gathered, waiting for your arrival.

You catch a glimpse of yourself in the car mirror, and worry that the left-side paralysis has made your face—among other things—appear misshapen and asymmetrical. Jim eases the car into the driveway. Everyone quietly watches as he takes the wheelchair from the trunk, sets it up next to the passenger door, and lifts you into the rolling chair.

The silence hurts. You are set up at the kitchen tables like a mannequin.

Mom and Dad actually start fighting over what food to make for you. Dad is bent on making a Brie, tomato, and pasta dish that you'd mentioned to him during one of his visits to the rehab hospital; Mom had prepared another menu. The fight feels far out of proportion to its content. Things are clearly tense.

On your wedding day you are getting ready upstairs, putting on your makeup, and you can hear Mom and Dad bickering about what sandwich you are going to have. Mom has made a seafood salad sandwich and Dad has made a roast beef sand-

wich. Diplomatically, you say you'd like half of each. You can tell they're nervous, marrying off their only daughter. You sit down in the kitchen and eat both sandwich halves and everyone calms down.

DINNER SEEMS TO HAVE BEEN EATEN, because you hear someone doing the dishes and find yourself sitting in an armless chair in the center of the kitchen. Jim has left the room for a moment.

Then disaster strikes. Your center of gravity shifts and you slide off the chair and you hit the refrigerator door with the back of your head before landing in a slump on the floor. The sound is awful, much worse than the pain. You notice that Rory is watching from the other room; his eyes are huge.

Jim rematerializes in a heartbeat; your dad had witnessed the whole scene from the same room. As Jim kneels down to you, Dad starts crying and wringing his hands, saying the fall had happened in slow motion and that he should have prevented it. Everyone is freaking out; they think the fall has caused permanent brain damage, or perhaps that you're going to die then and there.

Jim immediately wants to pick you up and put you back in the chair as if it didn't happen. But the jolt has caused muscle spasticity, making your attempts to get up rigid and awkward. You have to lie there until all the misfiring muscles calm down enough to allow him to help you back up.

You keep saying you're okay, that you simply need to regroup after performing your break-dancing routine. You have now learned the hard way, via the floor, and without any doubt, that you can only sit in chairs that have arms. Armless chairs will always put you at risk of falling.

Falling has become part of your life. It is something you can deal with. Your response is becoming familiar. Whenever you fall, people around you seem to stop breathing. They're waiting to see if you're still conscious. You learn to break the tension by saying things like, "I'm a master break-dancer!" You learn a lot about falling. Part of what you have to do when you fall is regroup slowly to give your muscles a chance to calm down. And then you have to check for any broken body parts.

A DINING ROOM CHAIR with arms is brought into the kitchen for you to sit in while Jim holds an ice pack to the blossoming egg on the back of your head. This formal-looking chair seems oddly misplaced to its environment—which is exactly how *you* feel.

You are getting tired.

The whole family is emotionally spent.

You realize, with some surprise, that you want to return to the rehab hospital. The place that you thought you wanted to get away from. The place to which you had assigned an unofficial anthem: the Animals' song, "We Gotta Get Out of This Place." You ask Jim to take you back there. Which seems strange, considering all the time you've spent away from these people you love: your parents, your son . . .

Rory.

Where is he?

What You Do Best

JUST AS JIM IS PREPARING the elaborate procedure of gathering you
back into the car to return to the rehab hospital, you notice that
Rory—who had been staying with your mom and dad since your
stroke—appears to be having some kind of weird allergic reaction.

He starts to wheeze and his eyes are getting puffy, red, and
watery.

Red blotches start to erupt on his face.

Rory was susceptible to eczema and you found that he would
get a similar reaction with dogs, especially with dog saliva. There
are a lot of dogs in your parents' neighborhood, and someone suggests that he had been in contact with a dog.

You wonder, though, what role the stress of seeing you fall
might have played.

Mom says, "I'll take him upstairs, soak him in a cool bath, and
give him some Benadryl and his allergies will calm down. Don't
worry."

She can tell you and Jim are worried. You think: Mom raised
nine children—she has more experience than Jim or you have. You
decide Rory is in competent hands and head back to the rehab hospital.

■ ■ ■

AT THE HOSPITAL, Jim gets you into your nightshirt, puts your foot and hand splints on, and settles you into bed. You are exhausted and you can tell Jim is, too. But you're still thinking about Rory.

"Before you leave, let's call to see how Rory is doing."

Jim dials your parents' number and gives you the handset.

It's really to make sure Rory is in bed and sleeping comfortably. You also want Mom and Dad to know you're back in the hospital's care and okay. But when you call, Dad answers the phone and tells you that Mom has taken Rory to the emergency room because of his allergic reaction.

You begin to hyperventilate as you relay the news to Jim. How much can a guy take in one day? Dad says Mom will call you at the rehab hospital as soon as she returns from the emergency room.

Jim won't leave your side until there's a follow-up call from Mom reassuring you both that your son is okay.

You wait. The phone won't ring.

Half an hour passes.

You say, "Jim, I can't survive if something happens to my only child. I'll be suicidal."

Jim thinks for a moment and then says, "Well, you might get suicidal, but I don't see how you're going to do anything about it. You can't get yourself a glass of water yet. You're going to have to wait until you're up and about before you get suicidal."

You consider this.

"Then you're just going to have to carry me to the open window and let me do what I do best: fall."

He stares at you.

What a jerky thing to say to the man who's going through all the same anxiety about his son and also dealing with the welfare of his wife. You realize it is selfish to talk like this when he is already dealing with so much. But your only child is in danger, and you don't know how he's doing, and you shouldn't have left the house, shouldn't have fallen down, shouldn't have gotten sick. You can handle anything that pertains to your health, but seeing someone else you love in pain . . .

"I'm sorry, Jim."

The period after the phone call to Dad makes time stand still. You both wait without speaking. Finally the phone bleats and you take a deep breath and pick up the receiver.

Mom says that Rory seems to have suffered an allergic reaction, maybe to something he ate, and that he is fine and in bed sleeping. Because of his reaction, Rory needs to carry an antihistamine injection pen with him now, because the next exposure to whatever substance caused this will be worse than the initial one.

Jim kisses you and leaves to drive back to what must be a very lonely house.

You lie there in a sterile bed, wondering what on earth you had let your son eat. Or breathe. Or see. You feel helpless, a foreign emotion.

You should have been taking care of your child.

Option C

AS PART OF YOUR REHABILITATION, the hospital suggests that while an inpatient, you go on outings to encounter what you will eventually have to deal with in the real world. Your friends Paul and Glenn announce that they are taking you, Jim, and Rory to the Museum of Science, which is a few blocks away.

Although the museum is quite close, you drive. Glenn becomes Rory's playmate for the day while Jim and Paul push you in the wheelchair through all the exhibits. You really aren't paying much attention to the museum, but more to the obstacles you have to contend with in your newly impaired body.

People are staring. You are the exhibit. This is what a handicapped person looks like. You can see people are trying to figure you out. Did you (a) have an auto accident? (b) fall out of a roller coaster? Or (c) escape from a psycho ward? Then you say, "I need to go to the bathroom."

Jim and Paul's eyes widen in terror. No one thought about this before leaving the hospital.

There you are, in a wheelchair, with three men and a child. At the hospital, you always have a nurse to assist you—or perhaps Jim could get you to the toilet. But how can you ask him to coordinate things in the women's room at the Museum of Science?

Paul wheels you over to the restroom entrances. He checks the men's room and notices it's empty.

"Why don't you go into the men's room and I'll watch the door?"

Not your favorite idea. You want to feel normal. You picture the likely environment. A soaked, urine-spattered seat.

"It's going to be disgusting," you say.

"How do you know?" Paul asks.

"I know because I grew up with eight brothers."

Jim and Paul decide to scope out the women's room for you.

While Glenn's playing with Rory on a space capsule (mercifully distracting him), you and your two companions are trapped by toilet etiquette. One woman enters—two exit. Three would enter, two would exit. Jim and Paul take it all in carefully, staring intently.

They look like perverts.

After ten minutes of watching and taking a head count, you have had enough with the whole hostage situation by the entrance to the Museum of Science women's room. You grab your cane and stand up, with some effort, from the wheelchair, and say, "Fuck it, I'm going in."

The guys are white and speechless.

You feel really wobbly, and it occurs to you that you must look wobbly too, like the Weebles that Fisher-Price used to make. You wobble—but you don't fall down.

You step toward the door, not entirely sure how you're going to pull this off. It has been a while since you peed by yourself. No one to hold you. No one to watch you. It's something you've been longing for, but suddenly it's the most frightening idea on earth. But you are determined not to let Jim and Paul see that you're scared.

You say it again, loud enough for everyone in the surrounding area to hear.

"Fuck it."

The people who have been staring at you all look like they've decided it's definitely option (c): escapee from the psycho ward.

Potty Perils

WEEBLES WOBBLE but they don't fall down.

You are upright, cane in hand, and purposefully pulling open the door and having to pee worse than you can remember at any time in your life and then a miracle takes place.

A stranger heading for the women's room door says to the guys, "Do you want me to help her?" Paul and Jim bob their heads nervously in unison, saying, "Yes, that would be great!"

Your new assistant escorts you through the door you've been staring at longer than any other exhibit in the museum.

There is a two-woman line ahead of you. You are clutching your cane as though your life depended on it. And maybe it does: You have not been out of the wheelchair on your own for more than a moment or so since you left the hospital. You feel nervous and weak, and you really have to go to the bathroom.

Your new companion is a little uneasy. She is studying you—your bald head, the huge question-mark incision, and the hospital bracelet.

"Have you recently been released from the hospital?"

"Yeah," you say. "This is my first outing from the hospital."

You see her glance again at the scar, and you're sure she's conjuring up thoughts of you being the recipient of a lobotomy.

"This," you continue, "is my first time out since my injury and I haven't gone to the bathroom on my own since my stroke. I always have assistance. To make matters worse, I'm having my period, which, I should tell you, really complicates the whole bathroom experience."

Her face is now the color of a cigarette ash. You feel you can read her mind; it's as if she were screaming, "Oh my god, I am going to have to go in there and wipe her and probably change her tampon, too."

In a halting hesitant voice, she says, "Do you need me to go in there with you?" She gestures to the handicapped stall.

Let her off the hook.

"No, I'll go in by myself."

Her body goes visibly limp with relief.

You really do need help, but you can't bear to put this Good Samaritan through much more.

You have great difficultly in the stall for several reasons. You are shaking uncontrollably from muscle weakness; the handicapped bar was located on the left side of the toilet, which is your paralyzed side—and you feel you're in danger of crashing headfirst into the floor because you're so dizzy. You're seeing stars, but you're not even in the planetarium.

You decide you are not going to fall down.

You remember that Paul and Jim are standing outside the women's room door, guarding it to make sure this poor woman doesn't try to leave without you. You can hear them laughing with each other; they knew what this unsuspecting woman was about to face. Of course, they may also be laughing nervously because they're afraid of hearing a big thud on the other side of the door.

You are not going to fall down.

The poor woman is trapped. She must think that if she tries to leave without you, they'll attack her.

You finish your business there in the stall. Weebles may wobble, but they do not fall down, damn it.

She waits for you to get out of the stall and then helps you at the sink. She sees you out the door, and as you settle into the wheel-chair with a plop you wonder if perhaps this is the last time she ever offers to help anyone, anywhere before getting a written affidavit outlining the specifics of the predicament she's inheriting.

The three of you thank her profusely.

She leaves, no doubt thankful to God.

You think: *I did it.*

Jurassic Meltdown

THERE IS AN EXCHANGE IN DUTY: Paul relieves Glenn to take care of Rory, while Glenn assists Jim with you. The two groups agree to rendezvous in the lower level, where the truck and dinosaur exhibits are located.

After a few minutes, Jim and Glenn wheel you to the massive *Tyrannosaurus rex* dinosaur skeleton, a huge exhibit that looms over you—over two stories of bones and sharp teeth. Paul, on his way down with Rory, learns quickly that *T. rex* is frightening to a three-year-old who can't distinguish what is real. Rory is instantly terrified of it and can't even look in that direction without screaming.

Rory works through the meltdown with Paul and reconnects with you, and the four of you end your excursion at the gift shop. Continuing with the dinosaur theme, they buy Rory a dinosaur rubber puppet. He really likes it. The four of you manage to make it back into the car, which is no small undertaking.

The car is starting to pull away when Jim checks the rearview mirror and notices the lone tripod cane standing curbside. You back up to retrieve it. Just like the wheelchair, it has become part of your newly redesigned, not yet rebuilt anatomy.

Paul and Glenn are in the backseat with Rory between them,

taking turns entertaining with the puppet. And then it happens. Rory breaks out into a blood-curdling scream. Apparently Glenn has made some kind of gnarling gesture with the puppet's teeth, and it terrifies Rory. He is hysterical until you reach the hospital parking lot.

After Rory has calmed down, Glenn asks him, "Do you remember who I am?"

Rory says, "Paul."

Without missing a beat, Glenn says, "That's right."

Thus it is that Rory blames Paul for scaring him with the dinosaur. You think to yourself that you will never look at a dinosaur in quite the same way again after this outing.

You had all planned to go out for pizza after the museum, but you're exhausted, physically and emotionally, and everyone else is just as drained from the whole experience. You opt to bring pizza back to your room at the rehab hospital. Paul and Glenn head home to recover.

You, Jim, and Rory have a pizza party in the grim, but considerably more manageable, surroundings of the rehab hospital. It occurs to you that there are many equally frightening exhibits on display here.

Brain Delayed

YOUR FRIENDS NANCY AND STEPHEN visit you nearly every day at the hospital. Jim feels comfortable because he knows that if there is ever a time that he will not be able to get there right away, they will be there with you.

This weekend, they are taking you on an outing to do some shopping. Rory's first day of preschool is approaching and you want to feel involved—even though you are going to miss the actual event.

Every mother wants to be part of her child's first day of school. So there you are at Copley Place, shopping at the Gap. You have bought Rory a few things that are several sizes too big. He most likely won't be able to wear them until he is seven, but you feel satisfied that you've actually bought him some new clothes for his first day.

Sitting in a wheelchair changes the whole shopping experience. There's no room for spontaneity; you have to go wherever you are led. After some meandering, Jim, you, and your friends decide to go for an early dinner. You agree to go to the Sail Loft in Cambridge, a nice spot overlooking the Charles River that's not too far away from the hospital. The evening is pleasant; you are out on the veranda. The sun is setting. Your head feels calm. This is a familiar place; when you and Jim lived on Admiral's Hill in Chelsea, you and he were regular diners here on Friday evenings. You used to cap off your week there to unwind and it was a nice segue into the weekend.

Someone at another table is staring at you. All day, you have been wearing a silly hat that your mom bought you. She recently picked up a bunch of different hats to cover your frightening head. You don't know where she got these hats, but you have fixated for some reason on this black straw hat with white silk daisies glued on the front.

It is a comical hat and you find yourself wearing it often. It represents the way you feel these days: ridiculous. Maybe it's better for people to stare at the hat rather than at your scarred, bald head. Maybe it's easier for you to answer the question "Why is that person staring?" when you wear this hat.

You make a mental note to save the hat for future outings. Or maybe Halloween. You are probably drawing more attention to yourself tonight by wearing this weird hat, and you don't care. You probably set some new trends while shopping at Copley.

What might they have said while you were shopping?

"Excuse me, what designer made your chapeau?"

"Oh, I bought it off the set of the *I Love Lucy* show."

AS WELL AS the hat and the wheelchair, you also have a sling on your left arm. The sling prevents your arm from flopping and keeps the arm in the shoulder joint. When you and Jim are with Nancy and Stephen, you always laugh a lot. You are apprehensive about laughing too hard with your vascular system on the mend—but then again, maybe laughing yourself to death is an acceptable way to go.

When the waiter arrives for your drink order, your friends order what they usually do. Alcohol is off limits for you. When your turn comes around, you want something other than ginger ale, which is pretty much all you drink at the hospital. You realize that you are having your first experience of socializing with your friends while they are imbibing and you are not. Nancy turns to face you directly to give you suggestions.

She sounds like she's speaking in slow motion, and twice as loud as usual: "WOULD YOU LIKE SOME ICED TEA OR SOME LEMONADE?"

It's as though she's speaking to a small child.

You look at her quizzically and turn to Stephen and Jim and ask, "What is she doing?" They both shrug.

You look back at her and say, "Is it because I look brain-damaged that you're talking to me like that?"

Somehow, this question snaps her out of her protective trance.

She starts laughing. Soon all of you are laughing.

The waiter is standing there patiently. It occurs to you that you will in fact have to order something. But you're still laughing.

"Pardon the interruption," you say, gasping. "I'm brain-delayed."

The table erupts in laughter once again. The poor guy has to keep standing there. Eventually you order a Shirley Temple.

This Party Will Self-Destruct
in Thirty Seconds

STILL AT THE SAIL LOFT.

It's a big help for Jim to have Nancy there to take you to the women's room. He has been dealing with all your needs on these kinds of outings, and at the same time staying involved with the medical care and being mother and father to Rory. No wonder he breathes this heavy sigh of relief when you announce you need to use the bathroom and Nancy jumps up to escort you. The two of you wobble off to the women's room.

When you return, you stop for a moment before you get back in your wheelchair. You stand at the entrance to the veranda for a few minutes watching Jim and Stephen talking. You realize that it's the first time that he has looked truly relaxed since this injury of yours took over your lives. Stephen has always had a way of getting Jim to let it all hang out.

YOU STAY AT THE SAIL LOFT for hours. It is so nice to be on the outside. You keep pleading with them, "Please don't take me back." And every time you do, you all crack up.

But eventually it is time to go.

When you are heading back to the hospital, you feel like a teenager about to get in trouble for missing curfew. It's as though you're bringing back your corrupt friends to face a locked door with angry parents waiting behind it.

All four of you are completely giddy as you make your way back in, as if you've been on a secret mission, and the job now is to sneak you back to your room without being seen. Actually, there is a reason for the drunken subterfuge: When you left for your outing, Jim had to sign you out and give both a time of departure and a time of return. Arriving after eleven o'clock means you are showing up several hours later than the time he logged.

So technically, yes, you are in trouble.

But somehow it's hard to feel that way for long.

Jim has to sign you in and get in touch with the nursing staff, because it's time for them to administer your medication. You already feel you've received the best possible medicine this evening, laughter, the medication nobody tells you that you must somehow administer to yourself if you want to make it through intact.

The Incident

THAT WOMAN down the hall is howling again.

You ask one of the aides to bring her to you so that you can see her face-to-face. She is wheeled into your room. She's young, just like you. You really want to talk with her.

Her aphasia makes it difficult for her to communicate and her paralysis affects her right hand. To talk with her you ask her to put her thumb up or down for yes or no. You can see in her eyes that she understands the instruction, but attempting to express it, she gets confused. Inside you are dying for her.

You decide that, rather than risk frustrating her, you won't ask any more questions. Instead, you tell her all about yourself, how you got here, what you've gone through, how this isn't what you expected. You talk for a long time. Two wheelchair women, each with an arm in a splint strapped to a board. You mirror each other like bookends. You're trying to see how much the two of you have in common that isn't already obvious.

Her eyes seem to speak to you, even though her mouth can't. She is listening very closely. You can see it in her eyes. You think you can see her soul in her eyes, too. There is no way you can judge her again.

You recall seeing this handsome, strapping man who passes your doorway regularly. He is taking care of her . . . forever faithful.

ONCE YOU HAD the outing to your house, you wanted to be home full-time. You kept thinking of Dorothy: "There's no place like home." That was true. But it was also true—the first visit back had convinced you—that there would never again be a place like the home you had on July 16, 1997.

> *An unrealistic wish.*
> *Only over time.*
> *As you evolve.*
> *Even if your body healed somehow.*
> *Not going back.*
> *Cards dealt you.*
> *Cards shuffle. They don't unshuffle.*

YOU OWN YOUR CONDITION—and you are generously sharing it with everyone close to you. In the hospital, you joke with friends and family about what to call what has happened to you. Some people think it is impolite to talk about one's illness. When referring to someone they know who has cancer, they will always mention it in a hushed, secretive tone, cupping their hand over their mouth: "He has cancer." As if this vocal trick lessens the impact of the illness. Maybe they're afraid that if they say it out loud, they may catch the disease. Don't talk about the elephant that has wandered into the house; if you talk about it, it won't leave the room.

Your friend Paul, whose family has dealt with a lot of cancer, leans toward black humor, a trait you love. The two of you hold a summit conference to determine what, precisely, you should call your predicament. "Stroke," you agree, sounds like something an old fogey would say; "hemorrhage" sounds too gruesome and too clinical, and anyway what happened to you is several things, not just one. Paul suggests calling it "the incident."

He always whispers the words whenever making any references to your condition: "before the incident," "after the incident." You love it.

You both crack up talking about "the incident," always pausing and saying it in a hushed tone. Talking this way is a great relief—it allows you a little distance, and keeps you from fixating on questions you can't answer or factors you can't control. For instance: What is it, exactly, that has happened to you? No satisfactory answer. On one hand, you are dealing with an injury, because there is a major wound to your brain. You have, in the words of the doctors, "lost a lot of real estate." On the other hand, you are dealing with an illness or chronic condition of some kind. What is it? Injury? Illness? Condition? You don't know what the hell it is, but you're living with all of the above. So you and Paul stick with "the incident." And you laugh. And it feels good.

YOU ARE SPENDING more and more time with the aphasic lady.

Your time with her is changing you. Your judgmental attitude is starting to crack.

Now, when you see her in the hallways, you always try to stop and look her in the eye. You touch her hand. You give her a smile. She looks back at you, very intently.

If you hear her during the middle of the night, it doesn't bother you anymore. You hear yourself saying a prayer for her well-being.

partTHREE

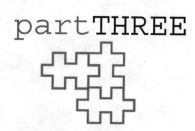

Beating the Odds, but Still Coming Up Uneven

A WEEKEND OCCUPATIONAL THERAPIST comes to work on your arm.

She has you lie down on your bed and tells you to try to hold your arm straight up in the air. Your arm keeps flopping on your face, and not gently.

She keeps telling you to put your arm up in the air . . . and you keep bashing yourself in the face. It hurts. It's like taking a club and whacking yourself in the face over and over again. Every time the OT lets go of your hand, it flops right into your face really hard. But you aren't going to give up.

"Hey," you ask, "how many people do you know who can actually beat themselves up and lose?"

You decide that if it takes beating yourself up for a while until you come out the winner, you'll stick with this strange therapy.

As you whack yourself, you keep telling yourself you only have some minor "deficits." Logically it doesn't make any sense, but it seems very important to you to keep reminding yourself of this, and the exercise is easier to do as a result.

Some minor deficits. Whack. Some minor deficits. Whack. Some minor deficits. Whack.

In the back of your mind, you wonder if this is delusional behavior, but in the front of your mind, you know you'd rather beat yourself up with a floppy arm than with an attitude that points you downward.

Your dad seems to believe you can will your left side to work. You want to buy into the same idea. If believing you are working your way back from a minor stroke—instead of accepting permanent debilitation from a major one—helps you push to improve yourself, that's the way it's going to be. That's a belief you're going to hold on to, even though you haven't been able to hold a thing for a while now . . . since the incident occurred.

A Pothole in the Journey

YOU ARE THIRTY-SEVEN YEARS OLD with a child who has recently turned three. You live in a suburban neighborhood, miles from stores, schools, playgrounds, everywhere you need to go. You just have to drive again.

Your physical therapist tells you that doctors are obligated to report certain conditions such as head injury and stroke to the Registry of Motor Vehicles. This, she tells you, triggers the RMV to review your license. They can decide to suspend it until you are completely retested—the written exam as well as the road test—to ensure that you are still capable of driving safely.

Your attorney-brother, Jason, reminds you that your driver's license is not a guaranteed right, but a privilege. He also tells you that if you don't comply with the stipulation to be retested, even if the RMV decides not to suspend your license, it leaves you much more vulnerable to a lawsuit in the event of an accident. Without the test, there will be no real proof that you are fully capable of operating a car.

One morning, Dr. Bleak appears in your room for morning rounds.

"Dr. Bleak, have you reported my injury to the RMV yet?" You ask with trepidation.

"Yes", he tells you, and then adds that you can take a test that will allow you to hold on to your license. He tells you that the hospital has a department to test your reflexes and administer a comprehensive cognitive test to establish your fitness to drive. He suggests you do it while you're here; it will be covered by insurance because you're an inpatient. After you are discharged, it will cost a couple of hundred dollars. Of course, you'll still have to take the road test before you can be cleared to drive again, but that's in the future. You don't worry about that now.

You are told that many people in your situation decline, for one reason or another, to take the battery of tests necessary to establish their driving fitness. Which means that if they choose to continue driving, they might very well be driving under a suspended license. (You will later find out that, in their infinite wisdom, the RMV doesn't necessarily notify you if they choose to suspend your driving privileges.)

You decide then and there that you are going to take the first test while you are still in the hospital. That will remove one more obstacle on the road to your recovery—a road you want to be on as the driver and not the passenger. In your current condition, you fear it is going to be like doing an extreme sport, but you are determined to win.

Your current inability to drive almost screams the word "dependent," a word you don't like to use in referring to yourself. You are aware that it is going to be a long while before you get behind the wheel—but you *will* drive again.

IT'S DOWN TO THE WIRE NOW, as your discharge date approaches. You insist that you have to take the driving examination before your release. The exam has to be set up with a physical therapist whose area of specialty is testing driving faculties, and those specialists are not always readily available. Since you are orchestrating your own discharge, you are adamant about getting your appointment immediately. Hospital staff pushes back, but in the end they relent. Your test is scheduled for the day before your discharge.

■ ■ ■

THE FIRST PART of the examination is a written test. In your case you are told you can answer verbally; you have to identify all the road signs. You have been driving for over twenty years, and now you are being asked rudimentary signage questions; it's a strange kind of time-warp experience.

Next, the therapist holds up flash cards, each representing a sign. You are supposed to identify each one.

There are some you know you've never seen before; it's not the stroke, it's just some weird squiggle from some region of the planet you've never been to.

"Hey," you say, "are you giving me the international version?"

There are approximately fifty-two sign cards, and she's holding up one you don't recognize. It has a lightning bolt shape next to a straight line. You have no idea.

She's waiting for an answer.

"Hmmmm," you say. "You are about to be struck by lightning if you don't toe the line?"

As it turns out, this sign means the road is going to narrow into one lane and if you don't pay attention to it, you'll end up in a ditch.

Supposedly.

You disagree with the answer, and you tell the therapist this. She starts to write some notes on her pad. You know that those notes, if she keeps writing them, can keep you from passing.

You stop talking.

YOU'RE THINKING, "Wow, I took this test when I was sixteen, and here I am trying to pass it again." Recalling information that you haven't accessed in decades is really difficult.

After the written examination and the signage flash cards, there is a physical exam to test your reflexes and your eyes. The test involves simulated pedals. You have to watch some lights and use your right foot to step on the appropriate pedal. One pedal is green (for the gas), another is red (for the brake), and a third is yellow (yield on the gas pedal). Your reaction to the lights is timed. Talk about being put under pressure!

You have always hated games that use a timer.

This isn't a game, though; your independence is at stake. You are so freaked out that you are a little afraid you will overcompensate on the braking.

The light flashes red—*bam* on the brake!

The time doesn't even register on the clock.

You ask, "Did I just leave tire tracks?"

YOU PASS ALL THREE TESTS. You get the doctor's endorsement that you qualify to take the road test whenever you are ready.

You have a long road of rehabilitation ahead before you will actually be driving on the road. You won't be ready physically or mentally to take the road test for months.

But something important is behind you now.

Steady

YOU REALIZE THAT YOU are getting the urge to go home, and that certain things have to happen for you to be discharged.

One of those checklist items is to have the therapists analyze your living arrangements to make sure that your home is handicapped adapted and safe. They're supposed to make a visit, but they never materialize for the home-visit recommendations, which (you decide) is just as well. You don't want your house adapted at all.

When the therapist starts talking about getting ramps into the house, making the downstairs office your bedroom, and putting grab bars everywhere, you know you don't want them in your house. You know what you need: normal surroundings, just the way it was when you left for work that day. Hopefully it won't be too dusty.

YOU REFUSE TO CHANGE your house in any permanent way. You do not want to have a handicapped mind-set; therefore, you don't want constant reminders of physical disability. You don't want to become dependent on any special equipment, and you don't want your family to feel handicapped by your situation.

It is essential that you keep training your brain to believe that

you will heal. Having too much handicapped equipment will sub-
consciously send the message that you are planning to remain disabled.

"I'm going to Rollerblade," you tell your therapist one afternoon.

You hear her sigh.

"You might consider," she advises, "consulting a psychiatrist in
order to get past this denial phase."

"Phase?" you ask. "What do you mean, phase?"

"It's stages of grief, except it's your body. First it's anger, then
denial, then sorrow, then acceptance."

"I bet you learned that right out of a textbook, huh?"

No answer.

"Well," you continue, "you haven't read this patient right, because one, I was never angry; two, I'm not in denial—I know up
close and personal exactly what has happened to me, and; three, I
don't plan on getting to the sorrow phase, because I'll be wasting
precious recovery time. So what happened, if you really want to
know, is I slapped all three of those phases together and went right
to acceptance. I accepted that I had a hemorrhagic stroke, and I've
accepted that I'm going to be a completely functional human being.
And I've also accepted that it's going to take a hell of a lot of will-
power and hard work to get there. Books are great for learning
tools, but the interpretation is up to the individual. When I read
a recipe in a cookbook, I make the dish with a little creativity. You
should try it sometime."

THERE ARE SPECIFIC PIECES of equipment you cannot do without,
and you resign yourself to them with the intention of using them
on a temporary basis. You will have to have a potty chair. You will
have to get a shower chair. You will need a cane. You will need a
wheelchair. You also consent to having handrails installed throughout the house.

You go shopping at the rehab hospital equipment showroom

before your release. The therapist takes you to the second floor, where you are able to try different styles and brands of chairs. This narrow corridor of a room is crammed with all types of handicapped equipment. It makes you feel like vomiting. Your intention was to leave all these disabling reminders of your new physical condition behind and to prepare for your escape. But here you are on the second floor. It's not as much fun as shopping for a new dress, but hey, at least you're shopping!

After practicing getting in and out of several shower chairs, you select the huge Rubbermaid model, the only one that doesn't skitter around when you grab the handle. It's so wide it can fit two people, and you find you're suddenly a believer in the "bigger-is-better" mantra. It certainly gives you more room for error when planting your butt. Your only concern is whether or not it will fit in the shower.

You have to pay for the chair out of pocket because it isn't covered by insurance. Guess the insurance company doesn't regard cleansing the body as part of your recovery.

You're required to pay for the chair before they will release you. You call Jim. "Hey, honey, I just purchased the most beautiful shower chair. I picked the designer model. I'm going to look fabulous on it. I need you to bring the checkbook."

"Should have known. No low-end models for you."

"It might be difficult getting it into the car. I got the wide-ass model. It'll be good practice for you in preparing to get your wide wife into the car.

"And, Jim?"

"Yes?"

"This is a far cry from buying me diamonds."

"What, they don't sell a Tiffany-bejeweled-throne version?"

INSURANCE DOES COVER the potty chair, your wheelchair (a standard model), and your cane.

Buying the cane is a bit of rebellion. There is the four-prong base, which is for solid support, and the standard single base. Which to choose? The physical therapists encourage you to get the multiple-prong base for additional safety.

You consider the four-prong base for all of one second.

You choose the single-base cane instead. You can't bring yourself to pick the safer cane; it conjures up images of nursing homes and sends all the wrong messages to your brain.

You look at the cane you have inherited through the good graces of your insurance company—it's gray, black, and ugly, the only one your policy will cover.

You quickly name the cane "Steady." He serves you well, and he has multiple uses: He is a good pointer, a grabber for out-of-reach objects, and, if necessary, a not-bad weapon.

He's scrappy, but he's got character.

YOUR PARENTS BUY YOU a Lucite cane for your birthday. They think it will make you feel better; it's prettier than Steady. You trust Steady, though, and you just can't bring yourself to trust the pretty cane.

You give it back, and ask them to give it to your grandma, who'll be thrilled with it. You're sticking with Steady.

Bodyguards

THE EVENING BEFORE YOUR RELEASE, your brother Jerry appears and says he has a surprise. He has scoped out all the handicapped access ramps in town and has found a nail salon in the North End.

Your brother Jerry is movie-star handsome when he's dressed in his business suit, as he is tonight. You, on the other hand, are bald and dressed in shabby lounge-around pajamas.

"Are you ready for your beauty date?" he asks. "I've got a plan on how to get you there." He helps you into your chariot. (You have started thinking of it as a chariot, rather than a wheelchair, because "chariot" makes you feel better.)

Out the front entrance and down the ramp, Jerry breaks into a run. He's pushing you fast. You love being on the outside with the wind in your face.

Just you and Jerry. Like you were kids again.

You holler out: "I'm free! I'm free!" into the wind as the city rushes by.

A guy in a nice suit pushing a bald lady in pajamas full speed through the streets of Boston. The pair of you must look like you're members of some outrageous cult—or possibly escapees from an insane asylum. People stare as you fly by. You look absolutely ridiculous, but it doesn't matter. Before they wheel you back to the hospital, you're going to have your nails and your toes done and they're going to look gorgeous.

As you approach the salon, you can see two of your brothers, Jimmy and Jason, waiting for you. Jerry slides you up the ramp to greet them.

The salon is tiny and packed with clients. There isn't room for the chariot, so you wait outside the entrance while Jerry goes into the salon and requests service for you. Everyone in the salon seems to be staring at you from the window. You wave gleefully to the staring faces.

You watch Jerry through the window. The conversation appears to be taking place by means of energetic hand motions. The next thing you know, the door to the left of the salon swings open, and you are wheeled to the back of the shop.

You peer forward and see a door—too narrow to accommodate your chariot. Through the door you can see a brown vinyl recliner with the sponge stuffing poking through its many holes. A sink is next to it. The room is tiny, dark, and crammed with jugs of various nail products. It is cluttered and claustrophobic.

"We're never going to get that chair in there," Jerry announces.

You correct him. "It's a chariot."

Jimmy and Jason lift you out of the chariot and fireman-tote you into the tiny, dark storage room where you are, you hope, going to receive the fully beauty treatment. Once you're in the vinyl recliner, you realize they've basically dumped you in a closet. Your brothers leave the door to the street open so you don't freak out. They stand guard on either side of the door. You feel like royalty.

Jerry is dismantling the chariot down to its smallest parts. You're not sure why, but it gives him something to do. When he was a little boy, he would take everything apart that he could get his hands on—clocks, toys, appliances, whatever. Once, Mom let him disembowel an old dishwasher after the new one had been safely installed.

While you're waiting for the manicurist, there is a frenzy of Vietnamese words flying back and forth in the next room. You recognize the nervous high-pitched voice of one woman, and start to laugh. By pure coincidence, the voice you are hearing from the next room belongs to the manicurist Jim had hired to come to the hospital to tend to you, the one who fled your hospital room in terror when you collapsed onto her.

You recall that she was quiet and withdrawn at the beginning of your last encounter. Now, however, she is a banshee, raving and furious. You don't have to speak her language to know what is going on. You figure she must be the low person on the totem pole, because she loses the argument.

When she comes in to attend to your beauty needs, she is obviously not happy with her task, her client, or perhaps life on earth. She stares ruefully out the door, where your brothers stand, arms folded tight and grim faces set cold. You imagine her thoughts. She tried once to escape, and thought she had succeeded. This time you have come to her—and with bodyguards! She is probably wondering why Buddha has chosen to torture her.

"Hi, there!" you say cheerfully, smiling as broad a smile as you can manage. "Ready for round two?"

You Shall Be Released

MID-SEPTEMBER NOW. You are about to be formally released from the rehab hospital. The doctors are careful to assure you that this doesn't mean, by any stretch of the imagination, that this will be the last time you see this hospital. It's going to be a part of your life, they tell you, for a long time to come.

But you don't live here anymore. You are going home. Not for a visit, but for good.

When the morning finally arrives, you feel like you can't leave soon enough. You can't wait for Jim to show up. You call him several times to say, "When are you coming? Please leave now."

He arrives about eleven in the morning and sets to work packing the car. After all your accoutrements have been loaded in, he slowly gets you into the car, packed up with your wheelchair, and he places two pillows under your left arm to keep the arm in the shoulder socket. (Your left side is so flaccid that your arm literally hangs out of the socket. Sometimes the aides who help you get washed or get to the toilet will inadvertently grab the left arm to transfer you, causing it to come out of the socket even more.)

You are excited about going home, but you are also apprehensive about the obstacles you will now face. You are a different
person than you were on July 17, both physically and emotionally. You are still getting acquainted with this strange, suddenly
foreign body.

Welcome to Headquarters

THIS IS IT.

Home.

No longer a rehearsal. You live here again.

You hear Jim in the other room. No doubt about it. You have made it back from the hospital. This is your life now.

There is a wheelchair in the kitchen, you remember. It offers plenty of open space, but mostly you will hold court in what Jim has designated your "headquarters," your leather chair and ottoman. It has your table and the phone and a pile of books.

That's the sound from the next room. He's cooking. Right.

Jim is getting ready to serve dinner to you at headquarters.

Where is Rory?

JIM TAKING your dinner dish away.

"Pasta. Your favorite. Be right back."

He smiles. He looks tired. A thought flashes. Whether you will be waited on for the rest of your life.

Eyes squeezed tight. He says something, can't make it out.

Open your eyes.

He sounds like he's looking for bowls. Looking for something.

Probably bowls. In a minute he will be scooping leftover pasta into them.

Do something.

You get up, trying to help him. You have a wineglass in your hand from dinner and you trip. You fall. Again.

He hears the thud and rushes to you. He carefully picks you up, sits you back down, and smoothes all your ruffled parts. He surveys you for damage. You feel a little like a potted plant that has been knocked over and then attended to by a loving gardener.

You survey the room. The red wine is all over the wall, all over the silk lampshade, all over the Tibetan rug, it's everywhere. Very impressive. It looks like you've just made Spin-Art with your family room as the canvas. You have created perhaps the most notable mess in your long series of messes.

It's what you seem to be good at now. Your body itself is a big mess. Messes are your specialty. It's your area of expertise.

"Jim, I'm sorry."

He must have told you where Rory is, but you don't remember now.

Bowl of pasta in front of you.

Jim has disappeared. You hear running water.

"I'm sorry."

JIM CLEANING UP.

Jim getting you upstairs.

Jim putting the splint on your leg,

Jim putting the splint on your arm.

Jim propping the pillows under your shoulder to keep your arm in the socket.

"I'm sorry, Jim. I'm sorry."

Jim turns out the lights.

You start crying.

"Jim, I'm sorry, I'm so sorry."

He kneels next to you and starts crying on your chest.

You both cry hard for a long time. Time hurts now. The house is the same but everything else is different. Time is different. You want to have another baby and you spilled the wine and time still doesn't work right yet and the pasta tasted like pennies and you want your life back.

He stops crying, but you are still going full throttle. Maybe the drugs. Maybe this is a mood swing like they said you might have.

"I'm sorry."

Your throat is raw from the crying.

"I never wanted to be so dependent. I don't want to make taking care of me your whole life. I'm so sorry, Jim. I'm not going to let that be your life."

Finally it stops. Your throat stops, everything stops. You fall asleep.

WHAT WAS IT that you wanted to think. Yes, where Rory is. But it's so dark. You can't wake Jim to ask.

You must have asked, he must have told you. Probably at your parents' place. But still, where is he?

Headquarters, the wineglass, the ruined lampshade, the splints, your throat, which still aches a little. And Jim asleep next to you, thank God.

Those terrible stains.

But what was that, what you wanted to . . . ? Yes, it was Rory. Well, if he weren't okay, Jim wouldn't be asleep here. Just be in bed with Jim now, wait, ask again, and next time you'll remember. You will.

Even silence is different now.

This is it.

Home.

Foreplay Takes On
a New Meaning

YOU REALIZE RETURNING to the house prematurely, which was what you did, was a selfish response to your misery in the hospital. You wanted to be home with your family. You weren't thinking how difficult it was going to be for Jim. The falls were harder on him, emotionally, than they were on you, physically.

It is going to be precarious for a while.

SUNDAY, the day after you arrive, a visiting nurse arrives at your home to see what kind of inpatient care you need.

You're expecting her to prescribe an aide to bathe and dress you in the morning, and perhaps to help with morning household routines. After all, there's a three-year-old to take care of, too.

For some reason, though, she only stays for a few minutes.

After the visit, you learn that she has not recommended a home nurse. Only occupational and physical therapy, and a few visits with a speech therapist.

A snap decision.

Or is it? The insurance company is unwilling to offer home

nursing unless there is no other avenue for household needs. In other words, if you have relatives, you don't need a nurse.

It's a cost-saving measure for the insurance company, but a decision that puts even more of a burden on Jim.

Somehow, you didn't think that was possible. But obviously it is.

THIS IS YOUR new regular morning routine:

Jim puts a sock, brace, and sneaker on your left foot.

Jim puts a sock and sneaker on your right foot.

Jim helps you into the bathroom.

Jim gets you into the tub, seated on the shower chair.

Jim removes the sneakers, socks, and brace.

Jim washes your face and bathes your body.

Jim holds your left arm over your head and shaves your underarm.

You hold your right arm over your head while Jim shaves your right underarm.

Jim shaves your legs.

Jim washes your hair.

Jim hoses you down.

Jim towels you dry.

Jim puts the socks, the brace, and the sneakers back on to move you back to the bedside.

Jim removes the socks, the brace, and the sneakers once again, so as to begin the process of putting clothes on you.

THIS MORNING, Jim is dressing you. He is threading your legs through your underwear and then threading your legs into pants. To pull the pants all the way up, he has to lift you up while holding onto the waistband of the pants.

As you're hoisted in midair, you remark: "I never thought you'd be working so hard to put my pants on. In the old days, you'd be trying to get them off!"

The top comes next. He takes your dead-weight left arm first and threads it through the sleeve, then puts your right arm through the other sleeve, then pulls the top down over your head. Your arm flops to the side and dangles off the bed.

"This is a strange new dance. I'm having a hard time letting you take the lead. Perhaps you might want to get a new partner," you say as he plops you on the bed.

Then the socks again. As you watch him put your socks on your feet for the fourth time in less than an hour, you realize he is drawing them over your feet in exactly the way one would place socks on a sleeping infant, scrunching them over lifeless toes.

Here come the brace and the sneakers again.

Now it's time for him to dress Rory—who is still in diapers. You had been trying to potty-train him, and you were close to success, but he regressed and reverted to the diapers after your hemorrhage.

As you watch him, you realize that it's a good deal easier for him to dress a squirming three-year-old than it is for him to dress his wife.

ONCE HE'S DONE DRESSING those two distinctly uncooperative bodies, Jim is finally ready to get himself dressed and ready for work.

A kiss good-bye. The sound of his car in the driveway, then easing into the street outside. Then gone.

He is on his way to work.

WHEN HE COMES HOME TONIGHT, it will be time to get both of you ready for bed so he can face another morning just like this one.

After changing two very dependent and (not infrequently) messy family members, Jim must think it's peace on earth to get caught in the rush-hour commute. Once upon a time, the stop-and-go drive would have been stressful. Now, you hope, it's an escape. You hope work is a break and a distraction for him, but then you stop and wonder how it can be.

You don't know how he manages to remain as calm as he does.

He always expresses love while performing caretaking duties for you.

You resolve that he will not have this nurse's aide position in your marriage for long. You want him to remain married to you because he's happy, not because he feels trapped.

You remember Paul joking with you at the hospital.

"Geez, Jim is really screwed now."

"Why?"

"Because if he left his sick, paralyzed wife, he'd really look like an asshole. Your family would put a contract out on him."

You both laughed. Now, though, recalling it, you feel the wave of sadness underneath the joke. Is Jim really stuck?

ONE MORNING, before Jim leaves for work, you ask him whether he still would have married you if he had known what was going to happen. It is a loaded question and not a fair one. If he answers "Of course, absolutely," you'll both know it isn't true.

He waves it off. "It's the kind of question that really can't be posed or answered," he says, smiling.

He's your rock.

YOU WORK OUT A SCHEDULE where your mother will take care of you at home while Jim works. According to the doctors, you can never be alone. You need twenty-four-hour care. You and Jim also have Rory in preschool three mornings a week, and he needs to be driven to and from school.

One evening, your mom has to leave an hour earlier than usual. You want to give Rory his dinner. Mom thinks you should wait until Jim makes it back before you eat.

"I want to give him dinner, Mom."

She looks at you uneasily.

"Relax, Mom. Jim will be home soon."

Mom heats some pasta and sauce for you before leaving. She kisses you good-bye.

She's gone.

This is it.

You're home.

"Hungry, Rory?"

YOU WHEEL OVER to his high chair. Mom has set the pasta on a stool next to you. Using one hand, you dip the spoon in the pasta. It flips over.

The hot food splatters on Rory's shirt, on your shoes, and all over the wall. You look at Rory and he looks at you—sauce dripping off his face.

Fortunately, neither of you is burned. There's nothing you can do except leave it all until Jim comes home. You feel terrible that Jim is going to walk in the door and be faced with this mess.

It's the first time your mess includes your son.

SAUCE ALL OVER RORY.

Jim wiping up Rory.

Pasta on your shirt and lap.

Jim wiping you up.

Jim wiping up the floor and wall.

IN THE HOSPITAL, the therapist told you: "You'll adapt. You'll find new ways to accomplish the daily activities."

You don't want to adapt. You want to get better. You want to be the person you were before July 17. You are going to go back to work. You and Jim are going to have another baby. This life is going to be new and good for both of you.

You need lofty goals. If you have a good, tough goal, you'll work harder. That's always been your way. You are a work-in-progress that will always be in the to-do box. Everyone faces challenges in life. Change is continuous and we are constantly adapting. For you, it is not denial. It is survival. We all have been given the power within us to overcome any situation. It's our choice as to whether we tap into that strength. Great things don't come easily. It takes a lot of hard work and patience, and God knows, Jim has enough experience in that department.

When is the good stuff going to be sent in his direction? Instead of an endless series of messes?

Can You Say
"Denying Denial"?

YOU HAVE A COUPLE of in-home sessions with a speech pathologist. The two of you don't connect very well, and you don't get a lot out of the sessions. You don't get the feeling she likes you. Her face puckers like she ate a sour lemon every time she talks to you.

The occupational therapist will be able to spend a lot more time with you. The OT, the doctors explained before you left the rehab hospital, is supposed to teach you how to get around your house and adapt to your own body, to regain normal functioning.

But what is "normal"?

THE OT IS FIFTYISH, has auburn-gray hair, and a wide butt. Her overall body is horizontally challenged and reminds you of a nun. The first session has been mostly awkward silences.

She sips a cup of coffee. "What are some of the things you expect to do around your house?" she asks, her face blank.

At first, you're not quite sure how to answer that. But then you decide you might as well go for broke.

"Well," you ask, "what do you do in your house?"

She looks at you like you've just told her that her dog is ugly.

"I mean, think about it," you continue. "Think about how you are in your house. That's how I want to be. I should be able to make a bed. I should be able to cook. That used to be my passion. I should be able to do any of the household work—cleaning, laundry."

She's still not quite sure what to make of you. She eyes you warily.

"Oh, I don't know," she says. "If I were in your shoes, I'd be pretty happy to be rid of some of those jobs."

She's a sneaky one. Happy to be rid of those jobs. Like it's some kind of advantage not to get your life back.

"Well," you answer, "I know that to an able-bodied person it might sound like household drudgery to do the laundry. But it is actually something I want to do again."

"Why?"

"To prove to myself that I'm normal. I don't want to be dependent."

"Hmmm."

Very tricky indeed. Like that's a whole answer: Hmmm.

Silence.

"Hmmm," you hmmm right back.

She smiles. "It's just that I'm not sure you've gotten your head around the facts of the situation, that's all."

"I'm in denial."

"Yes. That's one way to put it."

"You know, I've heard that a lot. About my being in denial."

"It's something to think about."

She cocks one eyebrow, like a friendly nun.

"Well . . . maybe you're in denial."

She blinks. Twice, fast. Then twice, fast, again.

"How's that?" she asks.

"I just think you need a little time to come to grips with the reality of the situation," you say, smiling your best smile.

She blinks three times, then bites the tiniest edge of her lip. "You need," she says, "to adapt to your new body."

"I realize I need to put in the time to recover, but I am actually going to return to being a complete, functional person," you continue. "I'm going to walk again. I'm going to do laundry again. I'm going to cook again. I am going to work to become as close as God will let me be to the person I was before all this happened. In fact, I'm going to become even better than I was before all this happened, because I'm never going to stop working to improve my body, and I've already improved my spiritual life, because I've seen what it's like to be dead. Now, as someone who hasn't had that experience, you may find that it takes you a little time to get your head around the facts of the situation. I realize that. Denial can be a big problem, especially for someone who's got a job as demanding as yours is. But I really think I can help you get an understanding of the real boundaries you're looking at in your life."

She is still biting that lip.

You smile for her one more time. "If you're willing to work with me, that is."

You can read her mind. Inside, she's screaming: "I've got myself a real head case. I wonder if the other OT would trade cases—a head case for a nice, manageable worker's comp case."

"I DON'T THINK I'm going to need a speech therapist after all," you tell Jim that night while you're both lying in bed.

"No?"

"No, I think I'm pretty much back to normal with talking. And this lady is not helping me cognitively. She either hates her job or hates me. Whichever it is, I don't like her attitude. I don't need help from someone who's showing up just for a paycheck."

You know full well you've lost some cognitive functions—concentration, multitasking—and you also know you become overwhelmed easily. Frustration has become a daily fact of life. But even with all that, the frustration you feel with this lady is real. You don't need her in your life.

You're well aware, however, that you need to work on your head just as much as you need to work on your body. When Jim takes you and Rory for Sunday drives, Rory (naturally) wants your attention directed to him—but this is stressful and difficult for two reasons. First, your neck can't pivot around properly, and it hurts to even try. Second, it is virtually impossible for you to separate the sound of Rory talking from the voices and music issuing from the radio. You simply have to relearn something you used to take for granted, namely the process that allows you to tune out one sound and focus on another.

On this afternoon's drive, after holding in this frustration for who knows how long, you lose your patience.

"Turn that goddamned radio off, Jim!" you bark. "You say you want me to feel good on these drives, but how on earth can I feel good if I can't understand a word Rory is saying?"

Jim obediently switches off the radio.

But now Rory won't say anything. The three of you drive on in silence for a long time. You feel just as frustrated, just as confused as ever. You feel like the crappiest mother on earth.

On Your Back

AFTER BEING HOME for a few months, still not knowing whether you are going to be alive or dead six months from now, you are settled in your headquarters watching *Dateline* and you catch sight of a woman on television who makes your breath stop.

She is about your age, and she is being interviewed because she is dying of cancer. She has a six-year-old daughter. She wants her daughter to remember her.

She decided to videotape herself for the different stages of her daughter's life: one tape for immediately after her death, one tape for the next year, one tape for the year after that, and so on. She knew she wasn't going to make it—even though she is a tenacious fighter and has defied all the constraints of her supposed diagnosis-survival time. But the reality of death became unavoidable, and she wants to do as much for her family as she can.

She discusses the various things appropriate to the different ages of her daughter's future: menstrual cycles, dating boys, college, getting married. She discusses the realities of her husband's life after her death, and the fact that he will probably get married again.

She actually wrote a book about how to put your affairs in order before you die.

Your eyes keep welling up as you watch, but you stay focused. You look at Jim and say, "Maybe I should videotape myself for Rory."

What would he remember of you if you died tomorrow?

Jim isn't crazy about the idea. You put it on hold.

SOMETIMES, during the many trips in the car on your way to the doctors, you discuss funeral arrangements with your mom. You tell her you want Talking Heads singing "And She Was," and Elton John opening with "Funeral for a Friend."

She squirms at these discussions, but she doesn't discourage them.

So you tell her that you want to be waked in your wedding dress. It's beaded from head to toe and weighs twenty pounds. "I'll be on my back," you explain, "so even though the zipper won't come close to getting past my hips, no one at the wake will know.

"It cost a fortune, Mom, and I loved it, so why not wear it into eternity? Plus it might help a couple of my buddies laugh for a minute, right?" Anything that sparkles, you're in love with it . . . typical.

JIM BOUGHT YOU a diamond bracelet on a day you had another round of chemo. You were completely miserable, and he knew jewels made you happy. He was trying to get you to smile. The only thing you could say was, "I hope you checked out the return policy, because I'm probably not going to be around to wear it for long, and I want you to get a full refund."

Nice move. Now Jim was miserable, too.

Now Lie in It

THE OT AGREES to come three times a week.

The plan is to work on a different task for each visit. You decide it makes the most sense to start with making your own bed.

You have always had an obsession about being sure that your bed is made neatly. It borders on fanaticism. You refuse to get into a bed that is unmade.

"Hey, I know it's weird," you tell Jim the night before the OT is supposed to show up and give you bed-making lessons. "But we all have quirks. An unmade bed can make a neat room look like a mess—and a made bed can make a messy room look neat."

"I AM ALREADY CLEAR on the basic concept of making a bed," you explain to the OT. "It's my body I need help with."

She demonstrates how you can make the bed with only one side of you doing the work.

First, you are supposed to take the sheet and pull it toward the head of the bed.

Then, you are supposed to drag your body over to the opposite side of the bed, and repeat the process, pulling the sheet to the head of the bed on that side.

You watch her uneasily. There really is a stranger in your room showing you how to make your bed in this incredibly awkward fashion. Wake up, Julia—you're in a dream directed by David Lynch.

She finishes.

"So what do you think?" she asks.

"Honest?"

"Honest."

"My first thought was, 'You've got to be kidding. By the time I finish making the bed, it's going to be time to get back in it and go to sleep!'"

"Okay. That's your first thought. But what's the verdict? Do you want to practice making the bed this way, or don't you?"

You take a deep breath. You know what the answer is, what it has to be, but this seems like such an absurd waste of time . . .

"Maybe," you say, "you could just teach my son, Rory, how to make the bed, and that would give me kind of a two-for-one deal."

"I don't think that would be such a good idea. I'm being paid to teach you."

"Well, then," you say, ambling your way over to the corner of the bed, "you'd better start with me."

YOU SPEND YOUR ENTIRE SESSION with her learning how to make the bed with half a body, practicing it. It takes you forty-five minutes of determined effort before the bed looks even remotely presentable.

But it's done. A little wobbly in the corners, maybe, but acceptable.

"There," you say triumphantly. "How's that?"

She surveys your work.

"Not bad," she says, nodding her head in vague approval. "Not bad at all." She's looking at the bed like an Army drill sergeant. You expect her to pull out a quarter and bounce it off the center.

She walks to the corner of the bed.

She takes the corner of the bedspread in her hand. She reaches beneath it to the sheet you laid down so carefully. She yanks every-thing off the bed.

Clearly, Ms. Inyourhouse-OT is testing you.

"Let's try it again," she says, with the hint of a sparkle in her eye.

You fight back the impulse to pick up the sheet and strangle her with it.

You try it again. And again.

"Hey," you say as you start making the bed for the third time that day, "why don't we have a toga party?"

YOU KNOW HOW to make the bed with half your body now. It's ex-hausting, but you are elated by the accomplishment. You're not going to break any records or win a spot in the Guinness book of records, but after a full day of work, you can do it without devoting an entire morning of your life to the task.

The workaholic in you has finally, finally checked an item off your to-do list.

Jim suggests you call up your mom to tell her about this achievement.

When you do, she congratulates you—and then wonders aloud why it was that you weren't such a fanatic about learning how to make your bed when you were nine years old.

"Hey," you protest, "I feel nine years old mentally. I'm calling you to be congratulated for making my bed!"

You may feel nine years old in your mind, but your dead-weight body seems to be whispering that it's really closer to eighty.

Recipe for Success: Ignore Authority Figures

THE OT WANTS TO WORK with you on your rigid left claw.

She has you sit and play with putty, sliding your fingers through cornstarch. The cornstarch helps reduce the resistance from the sweat against a hard surface. You play with the stuff as she instructs and do the exercises she demonstrates, but it hurts your brain to try to lift your fingers one digit at a time, independent of one another. You have to concentrate intensely to pull it off.

If someone had told you a year ago that it would take this much mental effort to move the index finger of your left hand, you would have laughed so long and so loud. Now that you've reached your first goal—to have a bowel movement in private—your new goal is to be able to flip someone the bird with your left hand.

MS. INYOURHOUSE-OT thinks making a meal will be a good session. You agree.

Your choice? A daunting selection: Mary Chung's spicy noodles. The sauce alone contains nearly a hundred ingredients, and making the stuff will require you to open many containers—one-handed. But the OT is game, and so are you.

Okay. You will have to learn to be resourceful. You have to learn how to use your legs to cook, how to hold things in your mouth, how to wedge bottles up against the counter until you can get at them with your good hand.

Ms. OT thinks the best method is to pour all the ingredients into vessels prior to cooking. You think she has watched too many cooking shows where the kitchen staff prepares all the ingredients so the meals look simple.

You're going to cook again like you used to, not like you have a staff at your beck and call.

"I'm a huge fan of Emeril Lagasse," you tell her as you wedge open a jar of something brown. "I'm not only going to watch his show again, I'm going to make his recipes. I'm going to cook again, dammit."

YOU ARE CAREFULLY MEASURING out twelve tablespoons of soy sauce, and it is going really really slowly. You are using your teeth to hold the measuring spoon. It's not too appealing, but she did say to adapt.

Then a lightbulb with the dimmer set to "low" goes off in your head. What percentage of a cup is twelve tablespoons? Aw, hell. You failed the math test. Just guess.

It's easier to measure by the cup than one spoon at a time. Hell, do it like you did it before the stroke. You always thought measuring things was for wussy cooks. You'd rather wing it.

YOU STILL HAVE TO OPEN containers and pour their contents into cooking receptacles. What a mess. You wonder how many people on earth have ever tried to get a cup of peanut butter out of a jar and into a large bowl using only one hand.

There can't have been many such people. Anyway, you're now one of them, and it's invigorating. It's like wrestling a wild animal.

And the peanut butter seemed intent on winning. You're pretty sure that you heard somewhere that peanut butter was supposed to be good for your hair.

Whether it's good for kitchen floors, though, is an open question.

It turns out to be a special, extended session between you and the OT on this recipe. Your choice of Mary Chung's spicy noodles as your first post-stroke entree is, with every new ingredient you assault, more and more clearly evidence of deep brain damage on your part. The cookbook assures you that the normal prep time for this dish is fifteen minutes. You extend it to two days.

But they end up being the most satisfying spicy noodles you've ever tasted in your life.

My Gait Ain't What
It Used to Be

MS. INYOURHOUSE-OT is followed by Mr. Inhouse-PT.

He is much more aggressive. He is the jolt you want and need. He is the missing ingredient. Mr. Inhouse-PT was actually on a hiatus from his job at the hospital. He will eventually go back to his day job. What was that? President of a hospital!

He has gone back into physical therapy just to take a break from the stress of running a hospital. His goal, he tells you, is to get back to the basics. You can sense that he loves what he was doing, and that he is enthusiastic about it. He really knows his stuff. You can't wait for him to come to work with you. Having him ring your doorbell is the same thing as someone saying to you, "You're going to walk today. You're going to get stronger today."

HE HAS YOU DOING floor exercises on the very first day. He is a superior cheerleader and great at prompting you to do more than you thought you could. He gets down on the floor with you, barking out the count and saying stuff like, "Come on, you're going to run around the block next week. Keep it up. You're strong. You can do it."

This is exactly what you wanted. This is exactly what you were looking for.

ONE OF THE REGULAR EXERCISES involves walking around the island in your kitchen wearing your Keds sneakers—and without a brace. This means you constantly hyperextend your knee and turn your ankle as your foot and leg flop along on the hard surface.

It is difficult, and it doesn't feel great, but the mere act of putting on your sneakers in preparation for this exercise now gives you an enormous boost. You remember when you were a kid, Keds used to advertise that their sneakers could make you fly. Here you are, a kid again, getting ready to fly with your winged sneakers. It's actually a dual-purpose exercise: In addition to the walking itself, you need to learn to tie a shoe with one hand. It's laborious, but you give thanks to God for giving you the ultimate motivation: hope.

Your mom is always at your house babysitting you and doing laundry and household chores while you do your exercises. All the while, she observes your sessions with the aggressive Mr. Inhouse-PT. You know she believes he's pushing you too hard. You assure her that you love his approach and feel good—even though all your joints hurt.

Whenever you learn a new trick, you call out to her like a young kid: "Hey, Mom, look at me! Look at me! Give me a piece of gum and then I'll be multitasking."

Despite your pride in what you're accomplishing, your gait is really pathetic. Several times during the exercise, your knee will hyperextend inside out. It isn't pretty to look at and it doesn't feel great, but it is getting better. As bad as it looks, as much as it hurts, it is better than it was yesterday.

Balancing Act

THE PHYSICAL THERAPIST has put you next to the sink to do toe raises. Your right foot keeps taking over, leaving your left foot dangling.

It occurs to you that people don't realize how important their toes are. Leaving aside the fact that they are located low on the body, toes are shamefully low in the body-parts hierarchy. If you tell someone you have a broken toe, it doesn't elicit anywhere near the sympathy as telling them that you've just broken your leg. And yet, it can be just as debilitating. These seemingly insignificant body parts at the end of your feet, you now realize, hold the entire weight of the body up. They are what allow you to stand erect. If you don't have working toes, your balance isn't correct, and you can't walk. Your toes do a great deal to control your feet and to help direct the rest of your body.

You make a mental note to tell everyone you know that they should love their toes and treat their toes with respect.

Mr. Inhouse-PT sometimes takes you outside so the two of you can walk around the island in the cul-de-sac where you live. You are certain that you're quite a sight for the neighbors. You have a sling on your arm, a shadow of hair stubble with a big surgical question mark on your head, a castlike brace on your leg, and your cane Steady. You're walking like Frankenstein, except your balance isn't quite as good.

THE PT IS NOT actually working on your gait, so it doesn't matter to him how stupid you look as you walk around.

What he's working on is building up your stamina. You are weak and tired from your hospitalization and he knows it. Some of this fatigue has to do with the medication you're receiving. A lot of it is simple physical exhaustion from the hard work of trying to reclaim your body and your mind. It takes an enormous amount of energy to do the smallest task, like getting out of a chair.

The fatigue you feel is a major detriment to the quality of your life, and the physical therapist knows it. So, he's trying to help you build your strength up.

You have no control over the sudden onset of fatigue in your life now, and you hate it. You never took a nap before in your life, but now naps are necessary and impossible to avoid. You always feel groggy and drugged when you wake up from a nap. You don't have the refreshed feeling that Mom says "rejuvenates" her after a twenty-minute "power nap."

YOU ARE DETERMINED to get better.

You have a basket placed next to your chair. The basket contains different strengths of putty, a variety of children's toys, and a few sand balls for squeezing. The putty is different colors, reflecting the strength and resistance.

The OT puts pennies in the putty and your job is to work them out of the putty with your now-useless hand. Now, if she'd put diamonds in there, you would be a lot more efficient. One of the toys in the box is a block of wood with a series of holes. There's a peg attached to a long piece of string. The object is for you to thread the peg through the different holes with your bad hand. It's a toy intended for three-year-olds, not thirty-seven-year-olds. But, you don't care about the intended audience. You only care about getting whole again.

The exercise is supposed to help you with dexterity, but you find it extremely difficult. You keep thinking that you can will yourself to do it but you eventually have to admit that you have no power to pull this particular trick off.

At the very least, you think, it builds up your strength for the next day.

What Is Left . . .
Is Only Right

SPONTANEITY IS no longer part of your world.

You have to have everything methodically lined up and planned out with great effort and great will. You cannot just thread the peg through the holes in the wood. You must focus with laserlike concentration on the task and carefully issue orders to your hand and to your mind.

It is as though breathing suddenly became a conscious activity that you have to choose to execute, rather than something automatic.

In order to perform the simplest tasks, you must retrain your brain to be organized in the way that it no longer is. This is to compensate not only for your one-handedness, but also for your memory.

It changes the way you cook, the way you walk, the way you pick up a glass of water. You hate it. It makes you sad.

Cooking in particular, it turns out, is now an extraordinary downer. You decide to put the task aside for a while, with the intention of doing it at some point in the future with Jim. There are so many other areas for your body and your mind to retrain. Time to keep the frustrations to a minimum. Time to accomplish something so you can move on to the bigger things.

Time to try simpler tasks.

YOU ALWAYS ATTEMPT to open a door with your affected side. Your left hand has to do the work. That means it usually takes you several minutes to turn the doorknob, a job that took you less than a second and barely a thought in the days before your stroke.

At his tender age of three, Rory always waits patiently. He has a sense about him. This morning you, Rory, and your mother are headed somewhere and you are hindering the exit by trying to turn the doorknob on your own. Your mother and son stand behind you and wait patiently for you to open the door by yourself. Your mother knows how important it is to you. It takes you at least five minutes to get the handle turned enough for you to open it. Once you have won the doorknob battle, Rory smiles, turns to your mother, and gives her the two thumbs-up gesture. That simple, innocent gesture melts your heart and inspires you to do more.

YOU ARE IN THE BATHROOM, and you are standing there in the dark. You make a promise to yourself: "I am not going to go to the bathroom until I can turn on the lights in here."

You have been struggling with it for several minutes when Jim happens to walk past you in the hallway. He flicks the switch without missing a beat. You are stunned, because you were determined to achieve the goal, and he removed the conquest without even realizing it was your battle to win. For a moment you are angry, then the absurdity of your situation sets in, and you start to laugh. He comes back and asks you what is so funny. "Never mind," you say. You close the door and plop down on your geriatric toilet, which has a higher than normal seat and handles on either side.

■ ■ ■

YOU HAD OVER TWENTY VISITS each with the occupational and physical therapists. That is what your insurance allows before you get sent to outpatient care. Each step is a new adventure for you, and the question that is always on your mind is, What's next?

When you run out of visits, you do not want to run out of what's next. You are on a journey that doesn't end at twenty visits. You arrange for a visit to a local rehabilitation facility that, as luck would have it, is just over a mile from your house.

The Dirty Words

THE LOCAL REHAB PLACE really is convenient; Jim drops you off and Mom picks you up. Your first session is with a therapist who specializes in neuro injury.

You sit down with the therapist in her cramped little office and her assistant is there and they ask you what your expectations are.

You say, "My big expectation is that I don't want you to tell me 'no.' I want you to make that a dirty word. I also don't want to hear the word 'can't.' That's dirty, too. Unless you follow it up with the word 'yet.'"

"You mean you don't want us to tell you no, you can't do a certain exercise?"

"I mean I don't want you to tell me no, I can't do anything. That's not in my vocabulary. I am determined, and you should know that. Don't tell me so-and-so is something I can't do or something I should not do yet. I have been called an overachiever. I've heard that several times from therapists, and I know they don't mean it in a good way. What they are saying is that I overdo instead of doing just the right amount. So I'll admit it. I always tend to be excessive. But that is my personality. That is how I have always been; everything I do is always over the top. My friend Berbie always calls me 'Miss Excess.' I'm coming back now, so it's what I'm going to be doing in my recovery. Miss Excess. Or maybe Miss Success. Anyway, that's my expectation. I don't want you to ever say, 'No you can't.' Okay?"

She looks at her assistant. Then she gives a little nod and says, "Okay."

I know I sound like a spoiled brat, but I only like the word "no" when I say it myself.

BUT THERE'S A CATCH. You can do any exercise—but they get to say how many times you get to do it.

They give you a list of exercises and they insist that you can only do a certain number of sets. You chafe at this. You're trying to rush your body back to normal. That's your plan.

But while they will not limit your goals, they will not let you hurt yourself on the way to achieving them.

"The thing you don't understand yet," she says, "is that, with a stroke, there is no such thing as rushing. We'll help you get where you want to go—but you'll have to do it at our pace. We will not let you hurt yourself on the way there."

She waits for this to sink in. Then she continues.

"This isn't a to-do list. This isn't something you can check off. It's your life. It's going to take you a while to build up the strength you need. That's a fact, and it's not going to do either of us any good to ignore it. So you can't do the exercises in double doses. You're going to have to learn to build yourself back up. Slowly."

"The only thing I've ever done slowly in my entire life is wake up in the morning."

She just grins. Okay, it is one of your personality flaws. It is time for the impatient patient to get a little better at the patience game.

Going Nowhere—Slowly

ALL THE SAME, it is really tough to be somebody who wants everything done quickly and then all of a sudden is working at less than a snail's pace.

The first thing that physical therapists do is measure all your abilities; they mark them down and then they watch your progress. This is what they use to show insurance companies in order to continue your therapy.

And it is the insurance companies, not the medical professionals, that determine what you need for therapy. You are only allowed twenty therapy sessions per discipline, meaning you can have twenty PT, twenty OT, and twenty speech sessions for the year. Those are the rules set down by your insurance plan.

It doesn't matter whether you sprained an ankle or had a massive brain hemorrhage causing a devastating paralysis—it's still twenty visits. Or so the rule book says.

Fortunately, you've got someone who will help you rewrite the rule book—Jim.

Jim is an amazing advocate, writing letters, fighting with the insurance companies, and pushing, pushing, pushing. He always wins.

You certainly have a good case: You are still improving.

That's the thing when you're in therapy. You have to keep showing that you are improving. If you are still getting better, then you are in luck, because the insurance company says, "Okay, if she is improving, we can't let her go yet." But if you are on a plateau— even a temporary plateau—they say, "That's it, you're done."

So you are always pushing back at the therapists, focused on improving, obsessed with measuring your skills and proving that they are on an upward path. Your goal is always to get more and more done, to prove more and more progress, to exhaust every avenue for recovery you possibly can—so you can keep your insurance. You are completely driven.

But you have to do it s-l-o-w-l-y.

SUDDENLY YOU REMEMBER your very first day of therapy back at the rehab hospital.

You looked at the treadmill longingly and said, "That's what I want to do. I want to get on that treadmill and I want to be able to run again."

You now know that it would be quite some time before you could get on a treadmill. You now know that your gait would never be the way it was. But you do not expect it to be perfect and you would like to run. Not that you're a marathon runner or anything— you just want to know what it feels like again.

When they are doing the intake on you that first day of therapy, they had you on your stomach and they had you lifting different parts of your body. Your hamstrings were nonfunctioning at the time, and when they had you lift your leg while you were on your stomach, you couldn't do it, and the attempt caused your back to go into serious spasms. You threw it out because you had not done any exercises with your back. You had been lying in a bed most of the time and your back had gotten very weak. It is a common side effect with people who have had a stroke: When they start therapy, their backs get seriously strained.

■   ■   ■

SLOWLY. You are doing the exercises. And you are getting stronger. But slowly.

The therapist at the rehab center: "You're going to have to learn to be patient. We're going to build you up a little bit at a time. But we are going to build you back up. That's a promise."

partFOUR

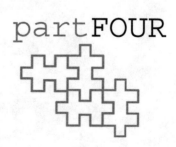

A Little Prick

YOUR LEFT SIDE is already paralyzed and not working, but your right side goes into deep spasms whenever the physical therapist starts working with you. You are in excruciating back pain and your neck is in a chronic state of spasm. You decide that you have to find other methods of alleviating the pain without increasing your medications.

It happens one afternoon, when you are seated in your headquarters, that you knock the big phone book onto the floor. You curse your spastic left arm, but then notice that the page has opened to the acupuncture listings. You stare at the book on the floor. You stare at your spastic left arm. You find yourself thinking about angels.

Then you pick up the phone, punch in a telephone number from the phone book, and set up an appointment.

HE'S FRENCH; he's been to China; he's learned all types of treatments; he promises to help get your body well. You love that he is confident that he can help. You sense serenity and a positive presence in his office.

"I recommend adding electric stimulation through the needles," he says. "I'll target the nerve endings. This will not only be good for pain control, but it will break up the tone in your muscles and stimulate some sensation in your nerve endings."

You trust him instinctively, but you're still not sure what to expect. "I have a whole body of pain problems," you say. "Am I going to look like a porcupine? Will I be so electrified that I could light a stadium?"

He laughs. "No, no. It doesn't work that way."

He explains the whole thing: The needles don't cover your body; they're strategically placed at particular pressure points.

"Will it hurt?" You know all too well that you can handle pain, but you'd rather not be surprised.

"It's going to be a little prick, then you'll feel the electric stimulation, and then you'll relax with the needles inserted for about twenty minutes."

"Good thing it's not a big prick. I hate pricks. Listen, what you just described sounds dangerously like sex. I'm not sure my husband is going to let me come back!"

He chuckles. Thank God. If there's one thing you've learned from your therapy it's that not everyone who treats you appreciates your sense of humor.

HE ASKS QUESTIONS—where the pain is located, what your medical history has been, how you feel about the treatment you've received so far. Only Dr. Neuro has shown you this kind of concern. You talk for a long time, you explain how you hurt everywhere, but currently your back and neck are in severe spasm.

"Julia, when you're resting with the needles, I want you to envision yourself walking—even running. It'll be exercising your brain and helping your body to remember. It's almost like physically doing it." You nod.

He seems wise.

AFTER A FEW SESSIONS, he can sense the different areas where the muscle tone is causing pain.

He puts tiny needles in your head that promote circulation to the injured area where your surgery was (a section of your skull had been removed and surgically reattached). It's amazing how it helps, but like the deep-tissue massage, the relief it brings is only temporary. If you had a localized injury, the needles might help more in the long term. A neurological injury is a different animal altogether. But even short-term relief is a blessing.

FOR ACUPUNCTURE treatment to work, you have to put your mind into it as well as your body. Going in for your treatment, you have to let the world stop and concentrate on the healing process. You have to remove all the clutter from your mind. You often hear people say, "Oh I tried acupuncture and it didn't work for me." But you quickly learn that you cannot go one time and expect a miracle. You need to go over a period of time, and you have to go with an open mind and not just expect that these needles are going to cure you. You need to make the conscious choice to put your mind and your own positive thoughts into the healing process. You can't just walk in the door for a treatment and then a cure happens. You have to work with the acupuncturist. It's up to you how much you get out of it.

In fact, you realize, that's the way it is for just about anything you involve yourself in these days.

Plastic Cup Blues

YOU AND JIM schedule it so that you have PT, OT, and speech therapy all in a row; that means you go in for the morning session and stay there through the afternoon.

The sessions are about forty-five minutes apart, and eventually include pool therapy, which you resisted at first. Getting into a bathing suit, you knew, was going to give you another stroke—not because of the difficulty of getting into the outfit, but because of the emotional reaction of seeing yourself in a mirror decked out for the beach! The bathing suit was an exercise in itself, and often you would have to rely on strangers for help. It's simply impossible for you to squeeze yourself into a suit with one functioning hand.

THE POOL THERAPY. Exercise in the pool, it turns out, is important, because in the water you can correct yourself without destroying your knee. Your knee really suffered from hyperextension, and stabilizing it is one of the things that you must work on constantly.

The calibrator. It tells them how strong your hand is, how much you can squeeze, how well you can use certain fingers, and how strong each finger is. The results are not good, but you say to the therapist, "Okay, that's why I'm here and I'm just going to improve on that." The therapists are blown away by the strength of your unaffected hand. They can't even use it as a comparison point for what the affected hand should be able to do, because it's stronger than that of most men.

The mirror. They have a full-length mirror on wheels that allows you to look at your left side. This makes the exercises easier to perform, because you can visualize what you're supposed to be doing and mimic your right side.

The parallel bars. Holding on for dear life.

The hand bicycle. It has pedals for the arms; you pedal the chain. Your hand won't stay on the handle, so they have to tape it in place.

The neck contraption. You lie on your back with a metal halo on your head to stretch the spasms in your neck. It looks—and feels—like a torture device from the Inquisition. But, oddly enough, it does help, and you quickly become addicted to this evil-looking prop.

THE THERAPIST makes you pick up pegs of different sizes and place them in little slots. The game is similar to checkers. You have to pick them up and place them where they belong. It's clumsy and uncomfortable, and your fingers are twisted like pretzels. You can tell that you have sustained major damage just by the awkward way your hand holds the pegs.

SHE MAKES YOU hold a cup of water in your weak hand and attempt to drink. You soak yourself. She hands you another cup. It's plastic, not paper, because your hand is so spastic it crushes a paper cup before it gets close to your mouth. You're enjoying this about as much as being the target in the dunk tank at a carnival.

"If I had known that you had this soaking exercise planned, I would've skipped the morning shower. Jim could've used the break from bathing me!"

■ ■ ■

YOU GO THROUGH a couple of replacement therapists; you could tell if they were innovative or not, and there are times where you feel like saying, "You're just going through the motions." But you keep it to yourself, because there are times now where you know it won't help your cause to speak your mind. You need each therapist to fight for you—to write letters to doctors and insurers and explain why you need more therapy.

As it stands, you've had a long hiatus from therapy because of insurance problems. You know that if you're not careful, you will basically fall into a black hole. No matter how good the chemistry feels, no matter how nice the therapist is, you realize that if you stop making progress, one of these people will write you off and be done with you. There is no real relationship—you are both at work. They may act as though they care about you enough to make sure you keep getting what you need, but you can't assume that's the case. You watch your mouth.

YOU ASK THE THERAPIST to test your left hand so you can see how you're doing.

She measures your hand strength once—then once again to make sure she got it right.

You're getting stronger. Pretty soon they're going to put your picture on a box of Wheaties!

Your Money's Worth

THE SECOND PHYSICAL THERAPIST you inherited is trying to discharge you from the outpatient program.

If he does, that means your treatment is over.

Therapy makes you accountable for progress, and that is what you want: to be accountable to someone other than yourself for making headway over the effects of your injury. It really helps the psyche when you know you have to own up to someone who can tell whether you have been doing your exercises by how much you've improved.

Today you are in the pool having your therapy when your primary therapist comes in and announces that he does not want you to have any more one-on-one therapy in the pool.

You look up at him.

"Why is that?" you ask.

"Because," he says, "you've had one-on-one therapy for an extended period of time and I need to make the pool therapist available as a benefit to others." It comes out so smoothly you know he's rehearsed this little speech.

About half a dozen other patients are staring at the two of you, waiting to see what will happen next.

"Well," you say, after splashing the water with your hand a

little for emphasis, "I feel that you are not articulating your reasons in a manner that I can or will accept."

You may not have rehearsed this, but it seems to be coming out without any difficulty.

"I feel," you continue, "that you should not be saying things like, 'as a benefit to others.' We are talking about my therapy, which means we are talking about *me*, and *me* is the reason I am here."

You're getting a little worked up, but so what.

"So," you say, "you don't tell *me* that you need to help *others* instead of me, because *I* am in therapy and *you're* getting paid as a result of that therapy. It's not that there's a problem with the insurance. It's not that the money isn't coming in. It's not that I'm not making progress. The problem is really stupid: I'm an inconvenience to you. From your point of view, I'm taking too much time to get better. Well, I have a feeling that some people are just a little too resigned to the fact that a patient has had a stroke. I have a feeling that some people are a bit too eager to get patients to say, 'Well, that's probably the best I can do, that's how it is going to be.' That's *not* how it is going to be. I'm making progress—you know it, and I know it. As long as I'm making progress I'm *not* going to say 'That's how it is.' Your goal right now seems to be to discharge me, not to help me get better. You know what that means? It means *you're not doing your job.* You're supposed to be my advocate, and instead you're spending all your energy trying to get me to be as apathetic about my progress as *you* are. But if *you* were here in this pool, would you be satisfied with the current return that you had in your legs? Would *you* feel like you'd gotten your money's worth before you'd learned how to walk again?"

His eyes are narrow now and his lips are tight. He turns on his heels and walks away from the pool.

"*Excuse* me," you yell after him, "I asked you a *question.*"

But he's gone.

The other patients in the pool start applauding, and the noise echoes satisfyingly around the water and off the walls.

Poof, You're Healed

YOU ARE WILLING TO TRY anything to get better, to go down any avenue if it holds even a shred of hope to return you to the way you were.

Nancy's mother is a volunteer on a prayer line and is associated with a priest known for administering healing services. He is scheduled for a Saturday afternoon service in Boston at a church in Mission Hill. Nancy says you should go; she insists that her daughter Alison had experienced the healing power from Father McDonough at a service.

Getting into Nancy's SUV, you realize that your body becomes very rigid, just like a stick. Jim picks you up like you are a log and tries catapulting you into the car. Mom is in the backseat and Nancy is in the driver's seat and you're being rammed into the car, the proverbial square peg in a round hole. You're laughing hysterically, which makes the rigidity problems worse.

Somehow he gets you into the SUV. With that, you're off to get healed.

IT IS A LARGE CHURCH and there isn't a parking lot. You and Mom go to get seating while Nancy parks. You find an empty pew in the front on the right wing of this cavernous holy house.

You have never been to this type of service and don't have a clue what to expect. Are you going to walk out of this place healed, as if nothing had happened to you? You've seen movies where that happened. You know it is unrealistic, but a piece of you is hopeful anyway. You expect a miracle.

Nancy approaches you. In a stage whisper she says, "Come on. Father McDonough wants to see you."

"We can't lose these seats, we'll end up in the back."

"Come on, come on. He's waiting for you."

You and Mom follow Nancy reluctantly, passing the front of the altar and heading toward a doorway into the vestibule. There are five or six other ill people seated with their companion standing beside each person.

Once you're in the vestibule, Father McDonough stands over each individual and asks why he or she is there. After listening quietly, he puts his hand on the person's head and says a prayer. The atmosphere is solemn. Once he has touched and prayed for each ill person, you all exit the room. As you exit the vestibule, you see the church is packed, but the very first pew in front of the pulpit is empty. You think there must be a "Reserved" sign up there for someone, but there isn't. The three of you settle into this pew, not entirely sure why it hasn't been taken yet.

Father McDonough stands at the pulpit and mumbles prayers over the microphone; the congregation is supposed to repeat after him. You can hardly understand what he is saying. He is so old and he moves and speaks stiffly. He reminds you of a robot. You whisper to Nancy that maybe he should go to a healing service himself!

The service chants quickly go to the background of your mind. You're thinking, "A few months ago, I left home one day to go to my job, and now, I'm sitting in a weird church in a tough suburb of Boston listening to an old guy drone on. I'm sitting here looking for the miracle that will make it the way it was before my stroke."

You feel splintered and the current environment makes you

feel like you have multiple personalities. You have to keep blowing your nose. What the hell are you doing here?

YOU STAY for the entire service. Three hours.

If you weren't in enough pain when you arrived, you are in agony by the end of the service. It's monotonous and you hurt. Some healing.

After all the chanting is done, Father McDonough starts going around the church and touching people, and people are falling backward in the aisles. Every time he touches someone, they crumple into a heap or fall backward. Maybe the miracle is that no one gets hurt when falling to the floor. Each person falls, light as a feather.

You don't understand. You think it's an act. You're dubious. You keep waiting for a huge thud from a falling body and whoops of pain.

When it is your turn to receive his healing touch, you brace yourself. No way are you dropping.

Father touches your shoulder gently and you stand, solid. He touches your shoulder again, this time with negligible force. You stand your ground, firm. He pushes you more firmly a third time, but the healing spirit, whatever it is, isn't entering.

You are ready to get into a shoving match with him, except he is so frail you feel you can blow him over and *he* will crumple! Inside, you're screaming, "Yeah, okay, you touched me, so what? I'm still wearing a sling on my arm, still have the brace on my left leg, and I'm still paralyzed on my left side."

You wish you could have shed the sling and brace, tossed it gleefully on the altar, run out of there like they do in the cartoons, thrown your hands in the air, yada yada yada. It's not happening.

YOU AVOID LOOKING around the place; you're not eager to see the pain of others. There is this one woman, though, who catches your attention. She is an Asian woman located three pews behind you, and when Father McDonough goes to touch her, she falls backward in the pew. You have watched the whole thing and you wonder what is wrong with her, and you can tell that she is with her husband and son. You want to respect her privacy but you can't stop yourself from watching. You feel like a voyeur staring into this woman's world and wondering what her illness is.

Mercifully, the service ends, and you head for home.

During the ride home, you ask Nancy how you came to be chosen for a private consultation with Father McDonough. Did her mom arrange for it somehow?

"No," Nancy answers, "it was so weird, Julia. Mom didn't even know you were coming. I came into the church after parking the car—right in front, by the way—and Father McDonough was in the back of the church. His back was to me, so I put my hand on his shoulder. Without turning around to face me, he said, 'Bring her to me.' That was it. Is that weird or what?"

JIM GREETS YOU ANXIOUSLY in the driveway. You realize he had been visualizing you walking out of the church as you once were. Maybe he too had been secretly hoping for a miracle.

But he takes one look at you and knows nothing has happened.

With mock glee, you shout, "I'm healed, I'm healed. I just have to wait until my hair grows back."

You glance over at your mother's car and see the whole front end has been smashed.

"What happened to Mom's car?"

Jim explains sheepishly that he had forgotten where her car was, and had backed into it, crushing the hood and grille. He's embarrassed; Mom had offered to move it before you left for your mission in Mission Hill. Mom drove away in a broken car, and you entered your home with your same old broken body.

"Since the healing service didn't work," you ask, "let's try this: Take me to the body shop and leave me there so I can get fixed along with Mom's car."

Coincidence Is in the Plan

ABOUT FOUR MONTHS LATER, you're leaving a local pharmacy when the same woman you had seen at the healing service approaches you in the parking lot. She stops and tells you she remembers you from the healing service at Mission Hill.

"Were you in a car accident?" she asks.

"No, most people assume that's what happened to me. Actually I had a brain hemorrhage and stroke that paralyzed my left side."

Normally, you would have made up a ridiculous story, like you were a matador in Spain and the bull let you live to spread the word that bulls rule! The look on this woman's face, though, tells you that you shouldn't make such a joke.

"Why were you at the healing service?" you ask her.

"I have ovarian cancer and I travel to attend as many healing services as are available. My son and I are going to Lourdes next week."

You can feel her desperation. She wants to live so much. Back in the pharmacy you just left, people are buying vitamins at the counter and someone is impatient about a prescription and the front page of the tabloids are howling about something a celebrity did wrong, but there you are outside, two strangers in a parking lot.

Life is bustling around you, and you're standing in a little bubble together, enveloped by your own mortality.

After you part, you think how strange it was to encounter, in your own hometown, the one person you noticed at the healing service forty miles away from where you live. Some people say, "What a coincidence!" There is no such thing as coincidence. Everything has a reason. The two of you were meant to see each other again. You may never know why, or what happened at Lourdes, or even if she is still alive. You may never know anything except that you both got something from your encounter.

Every now and then, you think of her and pray she has fared well.

Daisy and Audrey

STILL GRASPING FOR ANYTHING that can put you back in one piece, you try another spiritual avenue. Your mother had read about a young girl named Audrey who supposedly held miraculous powers. When she was three years old she fell into the family pool and was drowning for enough time that she went into a coma. She's now about fifteen—and still in a coma. People believe that she has healing powers and that she has created miracles.

Your mom is excited about Audrey, having first heard about her via word of mouth and then later actually reading about her in the newspaper. The newspaper seemed to confirm what she heard, so it must be true.

Mom encourages you to visit her and pray for a miracle.

Your internal reaction is, "Wow, this is too weird to be true. I'm going to hang out with a coma-ridden, fifteen-year-old girl, and through osmosis, I'm supposed to be healed!"

But you hear yourself say, "Okay, sure. I'll try it."

Desperation has this weird effect. It gets rid of barriers and leads to a new openness.

You want Berbie's daughter, Daisy, to go, too.

■　■　■

DAISY AND RORY were born two days apart. When you and your dear friend Berbie were pregnant together, people often joked that you must have been at the same party.

Berbie, being Rory's godmother, took care of him when you returned to work after taking pregnancy leave. Many people asked Berbie if the two children were twins; they each had healthy, chubby faces and mirrored each other in development that closely. Berbie loved to respond to this question by not answering affirmatively. Instead she would say, ambiguously, "They're two days apart." That always left people scratching their heads, and probably reaching for the *Guinness Book of World Records* to check the index under "birth phenomena."

When the babies turned two years old, Daisy was diagnosed with a cancerous tumor on the brain stem. She had emergency brain surgery and the doctors were able to remove 100 percent of the tumor. But this type of tumor usually leaves residual cancer cells, which meant Daisy had to undergo intensive chemotherapy treatment for a whole year. It was the same chemo you eventually had to allow them to push through your own veins: Cytoxan.

A month after her third birthday, there was a second occurrence of the tumor. She needed to have six weeks of full brain and spine radiation. This treatment caused her blood count to drop, and she frequently needed blood transfusions. She developed shingles, which required more hospitalization. Berbie and Daisy spent more time at the hospital than they did at home. Many holidays passed during those stays.

THREE MONTHS BEFORE her fourth birthday, Daisy has an MRI that shows that the tumor has reappeared. Having already used all the conventional treatments available, she was left to a course of treatment that involved experimental drugs. Her doctors tell Berbie that this treatment carries a projected 5 percent survival rate.

The Make a Wish Foundation arranges a trip for Daisy, her older brother (who's your godson), and her parents to go to Disney World.

The doctors are saying she should enjoy her life while she's feeling well.

The trip creates the illusion that life is normal and happy and wonderful and this is exactly what the doctors, and Daisy's family, are attempting to do. Smoke and mirrors.

"This trip, will it make things easier or more difficult for the family when you get home?" you ask Berbie.

She has to think about that one.

YOU ARE ADAMANT that a mistake has been made. You beg Berbie to get Daisy another MRI before she begins the treatment with the experimental drugs. You keep telling everyone who will listen what your heart is telling you: "It's a mistake. She doesn't have another occurrence of a tumor. They misdiagnosed her. I know it."

You say it so often, and to so many people, that Jim sits you down in the kitchen one afternoon and asks you a question.

"Are you absolutely sure," he asks, "that you're not saying she's misdiagnosed for some reason that has nothing to do with her condition?"

"Like what?"

"Like maybe you really want that to be the truth. Like maybe you want to believe doctors are wrong about this kind of thing."

You have to think about this. It's a possibility. Why *do* you feel so strongly about it?

And yet . . . does it really matter what your motivations are? How could it hurt anything to make the doctors take another look at their patient?

"No, Jim. I'm listening to my intuition. My intuition says they're wrong. Misdiagnoses happen. If they didn't, I'd be dead now."

WHEN DAISY'S FAMILY RETURNS from Disney World, you and Berbie talk.

Berbie agrees that it is important enough to check twice. She requests another MRI before the drugs with the 5 percent survival rate are administered to her little girl.

IT'S A FEW DAYS after this, following your discussion with your mom, that you call Berbie again, this time to ask her to accompany you to see Audrey Santos.

Berbie's of old Yankee stock—and she's skeptical by nature. You expect her to roll her eyes and assume you're suggesting a voodoo consultation. Hey, it's a strange request. "Berbie, I'm going to see a girl who has been in a coma for years and she's going to heal me, so let's bring Daisy, too." But she agrees, and the severity of Daisy's condition actually wins you a slot to see Audrey the following week.

Is it all insane? All you know is, you want to be the way you were, completely able-bodied, and you want Daisy to be well again, too. The way the doctors are talking, that means you each need a miracle. So fine—you and Daisy are in the market for miracles now.

The following week, Berbie, Daisy, Nancy, Mom, and you set out for Worcester to visit a fifteen-year-old girl in a coma.

A MAKESHIFT ADDITION to the family's tiny house is meant to be used as a chapel. There are a slew of cars parked in front, and dozens of people are lined up on the sidewalk. You wonder what the people in the neighborhood think of this spectacle.

Somebody comes out to check names. You're told that only one companion is allowed per name on the list. Nancy won't be allowed in and will have to wait outside. You and Nancy are disappointed, but you both know she will be among many other people who don't get to come inside.

The people standing behind you in line have been waiting over a year for this day, and have traveled all the way from Canada. Maybe there's something to this. Why would people wait years and travel so far if there weren't miraculous happenings? Why would television programs investigate this story unless there was some truth to it? The statues in the house, you have read, have cried a mysterious oil; the crucifix inside has bled.

YOU'RE TOLD TO SEAT yourselves in the makeshift chapel. There is a crude altar with religious statuary crammed in every available space. The statues have clear small plastic cups taped or rubber-banded to their sides, supposedly to catch the oil.

The room has several rows of metal folding chairs lined up all the way to the back. You, Berbie, Daisy, and your mom take the second row from the front. You turn to your mom and whisper, "I'm really bummed that they didn't let Nancy in with us. She's been by my side throughout so many things since this happened to me."

Then, to your astonishment, Nancy joins you in the front row.

"Did you pay someone off to let me in?" she whispers to you.

"No, why?"

"Because I was the only one in the whole crowd they singled out. I have no idea why they decided to let me in."

Weird.

The room fills quickly, but stays silent. It feels like children have been playing church and have put this room together. There is nothing sophisticated about it. You're not sure exactly what's supposed to happen here.

A bare-foot woman appears in the room. She is about five foot two and has a disheveled appearance, certainly not a professional spokesperson. She is Audrey's mother, Linda.

She tells you that Audrey is glad that you have all come here and that Audrey is praying for everybody. She instructs you on the procedures. You will go into her bedroom in small groups. Your group is first.

You move into a tiny room where there is a draped glass partition dividing the area. The ten people in your group stand silent, anticipating a personal cure.

The drapes slowly part to reveal Audrey in a hospital bed.

You're reminded of those old black-and-white movies where the newspaper reporter is witnessing a nurse tending to a patient. You're struck by how pretty she is. Her hair flows down the length of the bed and has a silky glow. Her skin is an unblemished milky white. Remarkably, her nails look healthy; you thought they'd be yellow and gnarly from the years of intravenous nutrition. If she wasn't in a coma, she would've most likely had braces for an overbite, but her teeth are bright and healthy.

Again, it strikes you that the girl is absolutely beautiful. You wonder if this is real or a hologram.

Her appearance alone is miraculous, given that she has been in a coma for ten years. You can't stop staring at her. You are mesmerized by her appearance, and you sense there is something special about her.

Linda explains that Audrey is aware of what is happening around her, but she chooses to remain in her coma. She exhibits the stigmata—wounds approximating those on the image of the crucified Christ—on her hands and feet.

As you stand in union staring at Audrey, some people start to sniffle and well up. Linda starts the group reciting the Our Father and the Hail Mary. You mumble the prayers, not really investing commitment. You are too much in awe. You have all these mixed emotions—you are confused by her and her situation. Part of you thinks it is a freak show, thinks her mother is exploiting her by displaying her like a circus sideshow. It feels weird to be in a group, staring at her. Why would this little girl *choose* at such a tender age to be connected to God with such confining earthly ties? Yet part of you agrees with what you have heard about her—that she had a choice to become cured or to remain connected to Christ, and chose to stay connected. Could it be possible, Linda was *sharing* her? Attempting to help people who have lost hope, giving them another reason to hope again.

You also had a choice.

You had the opportunity to stay or go when you fell unconscious in your hemorrhage. You suffered heart failure and it appeared that you had a seizure. What you saw was a white ladder with no beginning or end. It was a ladder to God. You could choose which end you wanted to occupy, what your proximity to God was going to be. You were given the choice to go to eternity or to stay. In this dreamlike state, you knew that if you chose to stay, it would be in a different body.

ON THE WAY OUT of Audrey's home, if one could really call it that, none of you has much to say. What you just experienced certainly didn't feel like a religious experience. Daisy is exactly the same. You are exactly the same.

As you leave, attendants give each of you a plastic bag with a cotton ball that contains the mystery oil. It's like a souvenir. As they hand you the little bag, you consider asking, "Do you guys sell it by the case? Because this one little swatch isn't going to cover my problem areas."

Is some unidentified oil really going to cure your shattered body?

Does it make sense to keep praying to return to the person you were before your injury?

You know you want to get better. But do you still want to be that person?

YOU'RE GLAD YOU WENT, even though you can't really articulate why. It could be that you want to be able to say to yourself that you've left no stone unturned in your quest to become healed. But now somehow that quest seems different.

You ask yourself, after this strange journey to Worcester, whether you should be praying to be healed, to be restored to where you were. Or should you be praying for help in rebuilding a new life in the body that's impaired, praying for the ability to accept this new life.

A sense of bewilderment sets in. During the long drive back

home, you wonder what the hell this trip was all about. You're pretty sure it had something to do with you, and with Daisy, and with Audrey, and with choice.

WHEN THE RESULTS COME BACK, the doctors call Berbie and tell her they have good news and bad news about Daisy's second MRI—the one you had insisted on as a double-check before the drug treatment began.

The "bad news" is that the doctors made a mistake in diagnosing Daisy with a recurrence of an inoperable brain tumor. (Berbie's not sure exactly how this counts as bad news, and neither are you when you hear about it, but the wording does reveal something interesting about how doctors look at the world.)

The good news is that the tumor, as you had insisted, really hasn't reoccurred at all. What the doctors had spotted before turned out to be a part of Daisy's normal brain structure.

Chestnuts Exploding
on an Open Fire

CHRISTMAS.

You want the celebration you had in the past. You want a big holiday party for family and friends. You want to cook everything, from the appetizers to the desserts. You want the gifts wrapped more elaborately than ever before. You want to share the Perfect Christmas with Rory and Jim—and maybe even teach Martha Stewart a few tricks.

That the holiday might really suck this year never enters your mind.

YOU ALWAYS LOVED walking the farm, examining each tree for the perfect A-line shape. You have been collecting ornaments since you were young, so the tree always has to be big enough to hold all those memories. This year you can't walk too much, though, and you have to take a ride on the cart used for hauling the trees.

DECORATING HAS ALWAYS been special, unwrapping each ornament and reminiscing with Jim on the origin. Making a game to see if he could remember when and where you got the ornament. Yet this year you are working very hard to keep from bursting into tears. You don't want to ruin the fun for Rory and you don't want Jim to see you upset. But each ornament now reminds you of something lost.

YOU INSIST ON A PARTY. Jim is like a chicken with his head cut off—running from store to store, grilling food, setting up the bar, and being one person in charge of fifty duties. You answer the door as promised, but even that is difficult. You fatigue quickly. People arrive and talk about how marvelous and healthy you look. They all want to make you feel good—everyone with the exception of Lil, an old family friend who has never minced words. She stays in the living room away from the other guests.

"Are you upset with me?" you ask Lil.

"Oh no, not at all. I'm not upset with *you*, dear. I'm upset with what happened to you. And I'm upset that people are telling you that you look marvelous. You don't look marvelous at all. You look awful."

Merry Christmas to you too, you think.

"Careful, Lil. You're going to give me a big ego with compliments like that."

But she is telling you the truth. You do look deformed. Your face is swollen, round and taut. Your eyes are slits surrounded by puffiness. Your hair is cut in the severest butch style, and you are dragging half your body behind you when you walk.

Jim always looks at you and says, "You're beautiful!" He means it. But what does he see—or *not* see?

CHRISTMAS EVE IS MISERABLE. You can't get out of your headquarters, the meal is burnt, and Rory is cranky and resists eating any of it. You overreact to his stubbornness and start to holler at him for his behavior. But what about *your* behavior? Who's the adult here? You have reduced yourself to the level of a three-year-old. You're in a headlock with him and you want to win. Is this the nurturing mother you once were?

The tension surrounds everything. The holiday puts your new and very different world under a magnifying glass, and what shows up isn't pretty. You hate yourself for being so impatient with his behavior. You know your anger is unreasonable and your reaction is irrational. Why can't you rein it in?

Because (the answer comes back silently) you loathe your condition and you're angry with yourself for losing everything good in your life.

The Ghost of Christmas Past is gone. Now you're dealing, uneasily, with the Ghost of Christmas Present. Not so sure what that third ghost has in store now.

Riptide

⊞

Narrow River, walking there, all broken glass and all snake-ridden, squirmy snakes, alive with them, writhing like a sea but it's all snakes. And Rory screaming. And you're supposed to walk through it and you don't know how.

JUST A DREAM.

You used to go to Narrow River before your stroke. Before Rory was born.

Narrow River is at the end of a beach in Rhode Island. It's a saltwater river that meets the ocean. It's about a mile walk down the beach and when you get there, you can jump into the water, and it will be like a wild ride that takes you with its powerful current and pours you into the mouth of the ocean. Then you swim back to the shore farther down. It's a fast-moving current and it can be really scary if you don't give in to it. If you relax and literally go with the flow, it's fun but if you get tense and fearful, the next thing you know, you're drinking saltwater because the water has its own will and you can't fight the will of the current, even a strong swimmer like you. And there's a moment of freedom, of not having to deal with any of your body parts in the water because you're floating and it's a really nice sensation. You enjoy Narrow River.

So before your stroke, when Rory was about two, you walked down the beach with Marie and Jim. Little Rory was on Jim's shoulder, and during the stroll Rory fell asleep. He was limp with fatigue and looked like a Cabbage Patch doll with his little baseball cap and sunglasses. When you got down to Narrow River, you just had an urge to jump right in, and you were out in the middle of the river when Rory woke up. When he saw you he started screaming, really petrified with panic. Marie was out there with you too, but you weren't even close to each other. You have no control at Narrow River—it's exhilarating.

And you remember being on that current and then, coming out, you get a little bit of a panic when you get to the point where you have to get to the shore. You think, Oh, am I going to get out of this riptide? But if you relax, which is what you do, it is just so much fun. So invigorating. Cool water caressing your body.

In the hospital, Marie sent you a huge bouquet of balloons—you always loved balloons; you even had balloons at your wedding—and the note she attached said, "Here's to walking with you to Narrow River."

Which is your goal now. That's where you want to go. Narrow River.

Now all you can seem to think about, though, is Rory screaming—and broken glass and snakes to make your way through.

THE DREAM: Impossible to get to where you wanted to be—had to walk there, through the snakes and the glass.

Rory's birthday party was five days prior to your hemorrhage. So now you have used the experience of that weekend to remember that it was the best Sunday you ever had. And who would have thought that? Who would have thought just having a cookout with your husband, and your son playing with his toys, a simple memory from a few months ago, would turn out to be the best Sunday you ever had?

It didn't seem like it at the time.

Who would think about the last weekend you happened to spend with your family as the best weekend ever? It only becomes the best weekend if something happens to you. Time and memories crystalize when something happens to you. If you're lucky.

Memories can become a heavy burden, a reminder of how different the present is. Even so, even coming out of a nightmare, you are glad you didn't lose the memory of Narrow River.

All Shapes and Forms

AFTER YOU RECOVER enough to use a cane, Marie invites you down to her beach house again. You have your doubts. Narrow River seems premature. You need practice before you can try that again.

You ask Mom to take you to a friend's house with a pool. You need to figure out if you can swim.

Your friend isn't there, but you and your mom know she won't mind if you go in the backyard. Your mother helps you make your way over to the pool area.

You take a deep breath, lean forward, and fall in the deep end. You tell your mom, "Don't help me out unless I don't come up for five minutes." Good thing you learned the sidestroke when you were younger.

YOU'RE IN THE WATER. On your own.

It's exciting, but a lot harder than you'd imagined, swimming with half of your body working, the other half dragging like an anchor. You're working like crazy, trying to keep your head above water. Your impaired sensation gives the message to your brain that you're swimming in Jell-O. You are quickly tired and sweating hard. It takes so much energy you can't believe it.

After only a few minutes, you decide that you're done. But there's a problem. This is one of those old-fashioned swimming pools where the ladder is hooked onto the side of the pool. No walk-in steps.

You try to master the ladder, but it's not the way it used to be, getting out of a pool. If you can't feel your limbs on one side, and you're weaker than a newborn, it's going to take a miracle to get you out of the situation you put yourself in. You would need those limbs to work to get on each rung . . .

Mom is more panicked than you are. She jumps in the pool fully dressed and tries putting your foot on the rung. It falls off. She wants to go get help but is afraid to leave you.

You are soon completely wedged in. Your leg is trapped between the ladder and the wall of the pool. You're like a block of cement.

It's not a good situation.

As events grow more dire, a strange calm settles in. You assume that you haven't been through all the crap you've been through so you can drown in a swimming pool.

God has plans for you.

A NEIGHBOR ARRIVES, with two children in tow. Her kids start doing cannonballs into the pool. They're huge boys, and the waves feel like tsunamis. Not big enough to dislodge you, just big enough to make you more exhausted. Neither the children nor the mother acknowledge you—it's as if you were invisible. Is this a dream where God is presenting you with another ladder challenge? If this was a dream, why is your leg bleeding and hurting so badly?

The neighbor is watching Mom's futile efforts to dislodge you. She is, like her boys, large. After about fifteen minutes of you and Mom struggling, and getting progressively more frantic (she figures she'll have to go get your brother), this huge woman comes over without saying a word and picks you up bodily, right out of the water. It's like being shot out of a cannon.

It's amazing. You had been thinking that it would take three people and most likely a crane to get you out of that pool. But she is not only huge, she is strong enough to lift your dead weight straight out of all the water that is pulling you down, too.

Afterward, you and Mom try to figure out how she did it. Mom thinks that it wasn't a lady at all, but an angel.

Angels appear in all shapes and forms. People probably encounter several angels a day without realizing it.

YOU PUT OFF NARROW RIVER. You can't walk on your own and you're not ready for the ride. But you do visit Marie and spend some time with her by the beach—you frolic in the water, and she holds you up, like a toddler. Every time a wave smacks your body, you tumble in the surf. If you go down, you can very easily drown, because it would be impossible for you to get up on your own. You envision the lifeguard coming to your rescue with his lifesaver and his surfboard . . . in a foot of water.

Thank God for Marie. People must think you're lovers, the way she's holding you.

There in the ocean water, holding on to Marie, you find yourself again thinking, as you often do these days, about angels.

Driving Miss Julia

YOU ARRANGE for a driving exam appointment on a beautiful spring Saturday morning. You are pacing (in your own distinctive, wobbly way) all morning, trying to shake the sensation that you may heave your breakfast.

You keep peering out the window, looking for the automobile you are supposed to be driving for your road test. Finally, a nondescript car pulls into your driveway. A hefty man walking with a slight limp approaches the front door. He introduces himself and then asks for your license.

You point to Jim. "Actually, I'm not the one taking the test—*he* is."

The guy doesn't laugh. This could be a long morning.

"Okay, it's me."

"Really. Never would have guessed."

It's hard to say what gave you away: The brace? Your big ugly cane? Your lifeless left side?

He cracks a smile. Thank God. You offer him a cup of coffee.

"No," he says. "Let's go for a drive first."

"How about a beer for the road?"

Not a word. He's like Mount Rushmore. That probably wasn't

the best joke to crack when your license is at stake. Damn. You wanted him to get to know you, like you, and pass you because you're a good egg (albeit a cracked one).

It's time to go. The thought of not passing this test, not being able to drive again, leaves you cold with panic.

Before leaving the house, you take one last, loving look at your license. You're actually fondling the thing.

"I'd better take that."

You reluctantly hand it over to Mr. Take-Your-License-Hostage.

"You'll get this back when you've passed."

Huh.

"What happens if I don't pass? Do you sell it on the black market?"

"Be positive," he advises.

You know the alternative to passing is failing, which means losing your license. What power this man has over you.

Be positive, Julia, be positive. Driving is like riding a bicycle—once you've learned, you don't forget how. *But I can't ride a bicycle now*, you think. That's negative, Julia. Be positive.

He leads the way quietly. You limp your way to his car.

IT'S A BITTER PILL to swallow when you have a privilege and then have it taken away.

You don't know what to expect. You can't use the driving exam you had when you were sixteen as a model of what to expect today. You were a cocky kid then, not concerned about failing. When you were twenty, the Massachusetts legislature raised the drinking age from eighteen to twenty-one. A literal raising of the bar! You had the right to go to bars for two years, but then had it revoked at twenty. Same thing here. Where's the grandfather clause when you need it?

You had practiced driving with Jim in the car, but not enough to feel completely comfortable at the wheel. It is hard to drive one-handed. You have to make sure everything is in exactly the correct position before moving—the side- and rearview mirrors, the temperature, seat, and radio settings—because you can't make any adjustments once you're in motion. If you have to scratch your nose, you have to stop and use your right hand—the hand you would otherwise use to hold the steering wheel.

You have no intention of buying a car that has to be altered by changing or adding special devices, for several reasons. First and most obviously, it will limit you to driving that specific car. You know there are going to be times when you need to drive Jim's car. Second, and even more important, it will send the wrong message to you and to the world at large: that you're disabled and need special equipment to function in the world.

But when you get into the instructor's car, he has a knob on the wheel. It allows you to turn the wheel around one-handed without having to stop and pull it again. No other hand movement is necessary.

You've never used one before and you know it will take you a while to get the hang of it. Mr. Take-Your-License-Hostage requests that you use it, because he thinks you will find it much easier to steer with. You agree to his request, but you don't really feel comfortable with it. You feel disconnected. But you pull out of the driveway anyway.

You have to use the weight of your whole body to flick the turn indicator. You wonder if you have ever concentrated this hard on anything before in your life. And your independence is at stake.

You feel completely at his mercy and subservient. You hate the idea of anyone having power over you. You feel like driving erratically, cruising onto the sidewalks, leaning out the window to yell "Road hog!" to the other drivers. *That* would be independence. Independence would be hitting the mailbox and running over the neighbor's lawn, but that would also be . . . well, impulsive.

And anyway, you don't want to piss this guy off.

"WELL, YOU MADE A MISTAKE when you didn't stop at the end of your driveway before pulling out," he says from the passenger seat after you pull back into your driveway.

"I'm in a cul-de-sac," you protest. "There was no one on my left, I was good to go."

"And when you were parallel-parking," he continues, "you should have looked twice before pulling away from the curb." This really feels like he's yanking your chain. You were at the very end of a dead-end road.

He keeps making sarcastic remarks about your plans to buy a new car. He won't stop talking about what an expensive car you purchased. Maybe he's jealous because his car—the car you're driving—is a seriously outdated Pacer.

You figure he is either busting your ass so you'll be really, really careful when you do get out on the open road or getting ready to deliver some bad news.

Which is it?

"But you're a very focused person, and I think you'll be all right if you work your way back up to getting out on the highway. You passed. Here's your license."

Whew.

There are a few restrictions: You can't drive a standard anymore. And he wants you to get one of those spinny knobs for the steering wheel.

"Actually, though, I think I'm going to be all right there. I'm only at the beginning of my recovery. I'm going to be able to use my left hand again."

He looks at you and you know exactly what he's thinking.

You look back at him so he can tell exactly what *you're* thinking: *I'm going to be cruising down 128 in a race car before you know it.*

Homage to Your Hemorrhage

ORIGINALLY THE PARTY marking your first full year of recovery is supposed to be a surprise, but Mom lets it slip. You tell her you're relieved to know about it ahead of time—you don't feel like a surprise party because you feel like you really have to process what you have been through in the last year. You don't feel like being shocked about anything else relating to your illness. You want to have some control over this process. If it were a surprise party, you'd probably burst into tears, and bawling will not be the best response for your family. So you look at it as a good chance to work through these enormous changes and not dwell on any of the negative stuff that you've been through.

The date is set: On July 17, 1998, your brother John plans to throw a party to celebrate your first year of recovery. You decide to call it your hemorrhage party, and invite your whole family and all your friends to come and pay "homage to my hemorrhage."

You joke with your sister-in-law about the proper way to decorate for a hemorrhage party. Should there be a lot of red balloons? Photos of your CAT scans on the wall? Recordings of songs by famous stroke victims?

It is a true birthday. After all, you were given another chance.

For nine months, you didn't know if you'd live out the year. It feels like a rebirth. Preparing for it and celebrating it means more to you than your actual birthday, because the stroke was such a life-altering event. You promise to celebrate your hemorrhage date every year, to celebrate in some way so that it is never forgotten. You don't take anything for granted. Every year, every month, every week, every second that passes is a victory.

THE DAY STARTS OUT with you doing PT, OT, and pool therapy; then your friends Nancy and Marie pick you up and head to Marble-head to have lunch at Oceanside. Then you head to your brother's house, where everyone converges for a celebration of survival, of life. You get eaten alive by mosquitoes around the pool. "At least," you remark, "I'm bleeding out a little less dramatically this time." Hey, you laugh at just about anything.

Jim says it is typical of you to want to celebrate the anniversary of your hemorrhage. He jokes that you can find something to celebrate in almost anything: "This is the first Monday of the month, so let's have a party." A month since MI (for moving in). Then there's BS for before stroke. And PS for poststroke.

The truth is, you also like excuses to get presents.

You get clothing, gift certificates to restaurants, all kinds of stuff. Your oldest brother and his kids give you a model of an exposed brain as a bike helmet. You wear it for the rest of the day.

Have Two Massive Mood Swings and Call Me in the Morning

PREDNISONE, a steroid you're taking, produces a Jekyll-and-Hyde effect. One minute, you're loving and understanding with Jim, and the next you're calling him names for reasons you don't really understand. Tonight you lost it because you didn't like the amount of food he put on your plate. You were having Chinese food and he gave you more rice than you wanted and you started screaming.

Or in the car with your mother. She takes you to all your doctor appointments and therapies, a task that has become a full-time job. You find yourself in the passenger seat gritting your teeth and agitated because she parked in a different parking spot than the one you had silently chosen. You're aware that your anger isn't rational, but you can't help it: You're pissed.

One Saturday morning, you can't bring yourself to get out of bed. Jim hears you weeping, comes into the bedroom, and lies down next to you.

"What's wrong?"

"I don't feel like myself. I don't want to get up and face another day in this damaged body. Everything is so hard and I'm just tired of trying to do basic shit, like getting dressed. I just don't think I can live this way. I can't do it."

"Can't do what? Get dressed? Come on, I'll help you."

"No, I don't think I can do all the things I keep telling everyone I'm going to do. I think I've been saying I'm going to do all this stuff to convince myself. Jim, I can't even put a sock on."

This is not who you are. You feel even worse now, because you've unloaded all your fears and insecurities on Jim. All he wants is positive energy from you, and you can't even give him that.

SOMEONE WHO IS on antiseizure medicine has to maintain a certain level of the drug for it to be effective. Blood tests have to be done regularly to ensure that the right level is maintained. If the level drops too far, the drug can actually *bring on* a seizure because the person's body is used to a certain amount of the drug.

The regular blood draws are a pain—you have tiny veins and lots of scar tissue. You're what the experts call "a tough stick."

The first and only time you gave blood to the Red Cross, they pinched a nerve and you had to wear a sling for two weeks. When you and Jim went for your marriage license, the nurse simply couldn't find your veins. You were stuck several times and then the nurse checked to see if the small amount drawn was acceptable. There wasn't enough and it all had to be done again.

"Jim," you say, "you've always been my rock, but now I'm starting to think *I'm* the rock, because you can't get blood out of a stone, and nobody can get any blood out of me."

Now Rory goes with you when you need to have a level check. He holds your hand while they find the vein and draw the blood. He is inquisitive and, as a toddler, part of his mother's support system.

You hate the blood draws. But you don't hate them as much as you hate the dependency. You don't want a synthetic wellness. You want to be free of any controlling dependencies: antiseizure medication, antispasm drugs, everything except the prenatal vitamins Dr. Neuro prescribed, the only drug that represents something good for you in your future.

During your neurology appointment, you ask Dr. Neuro flat out: "How are we going to reduce my drug intake?"

No answer.

"I want my life back," you continue, "and I am not going to let any drug have power over me."

"Whoa," Jim interjects, "before we discuss intake reduction, I'd like to point out an episode Julia had last weekend. She hit rock bottom with her mood. She was very depressed. I've known her over fifteen years and I've never seen her that low even when it's justifiable. It seems like something has changed."

You nod affirmatively.

"Depression is typical with stroke patients," Dr. Neuro explains, "and particularly with right-hemisphere stroke. Science hasn't yet figured out if it's a result of the assault to the brain or the disability the patient is left to deal with—usually it's both."

"I'm not suffering from depression. I've just lost some of my motivation because everything I do is so damn hard and I'm exhausted attempting to do the simplest task. And I thought depression was hereditary—no one suffers from depression in my family," you say defensively. The D word makes you bristle.

"I'm aware that you have no family history of depression but it's possible you are suffering from depression now. Your mood has been excellent throughout your recovery, and with a sudden onset of despair, I'm led to believe you have a serious chemical imbalance due to all the damaged brain cells. I think we should try putting you on an antidepressant," Dr. Neuro explains.

At the mention of another drug, and an antidepressant one, you are resistant. You're aware of the stigma attached to the word "depression." People perceive it as a weakness. You just want to feel like your old self emotionally. After considering how you feel, you know the real weakness would be *not* resolving a problem that's fixable.

Resigned to the fact that you need to do something to correct this sudden foreign feeling of being overwhelmed, you agree to try it. "Okay, I know I need to fix this and I'll take what you recommend, but I still want to reduce the other drugs. I don't feel that I need to remain on the antiseizure medicine.

"How about a trade—you wean me off the seizure medication, and I start the antidepressants? One antidrug for another antidrug. How's that for upping the ante!"

Dr. Neuro smiles. "That's the Julia I know. Let's keep her around. Deal?"

He starts shuffling through your charts and papers.

HE SAYS HE'LL wean you off the stuff, but he warns that it isn't simply a matter of not taking the pills. In his office there is a poster showing the requirements in every state for patients on antiseizure medicine: When there are changes to your dosage, you have to follow your state's laws, particularly regarding driving.

He goes through the whole discussion. You listen politely. You have been on this medicine for more than a year. You have to gradually reduce it over a period of six months, which is what Massachusetts requires.

You won't be able to drive for six months.

"Can I just move to a state that doesn't have a waiting period?" you ask.

He doesn't laugh. He says, "You really *must* follow these rules. Just recently one of my patients ignored the rules and started driving anyway. He had a serious accident, and he's in the middle of a messy, expensive lawsuit. Six months. No joke."

Now you're not laughing.

"Fine. Six months."

He says okay and starts to leave.

"Doctor, I want you to know something. I am going to start removing things that are controlling my life. And this drug is one of those things. And P.S., I'm going to have a baby."

He says, "I just want *you* to know something. If there's a problem, we have to put you back on the drug."

A little voice inside you says, "Don't worry. You're not going to have a seizure."

You trust that voice.

He leaves. It's January. You want to be driving by the end of June.

Bright Lights, Big Electrodes

DR. NEURO, squeamish that you could be sued, requests that you do a test so he can monitor your brain wave activity before you take any steps to wean yourself off the antiseizure medicine. This test will bring on a seizure if you're prone to them.

Which you're not.

But Dr. Neuro is cautious on this point, and you trust him (literally) with your life. So you do it his way.

USUALLY WHEN YOU are preparing for an exam, you're always told to get a good night's rest. This test requires the opposite—sleep deprivation. You are told to get no more than three hours of sleep the night before the test. Back in your college years, it wouldn't have been a big deal. Now, though, you feel like you're eighty. You need your sleep.

You're a creature of habit and you fall asleep at the same time every night. Usually, you doze off in your headquarters and are startled awake by something or other; then you drag yourself to bed.

Jim stops at the video store to pick up a movie for you to watch late into the wee hours. *Lethal Weapon 4*. Lots of action. Hard to sleep through.

You pop the movie in after midnight and settle in.

You're instructed not to have anything to eat or drink after midnight. At the stroke (there's that word again) of midnight, you are, of course, suffering from starvation and dehydration.

You stare at the television. Things explode.

IT IS PAST 3:30 when you finally stagger to bed. You are agitated from the movie, overtired, and anxious about the test tomorrow.

You don't sleep.

The next morning your mother drives you to the hospital. The nurse remembers you from intensive care. She's been transferred to the very department where your sleep habits will be studied. She says she never forgot you because you helped her learn that Things Happen, even to young people.

The electrodes are attached to different areas on your head. They scrape your scalp vigorously with sandpaper. This is to remove any substance that could interfere with a good electrode connection.

"Hey," you complain, "you're breaking my hair follicles—and I don't have that many to spare!"

The abuse continues. You catch a look at yourself. You look like Medusa.

They lead you to a closet of a room. There is a bed against the wall and next to it is a desk with a computer where a technician sits. He monitors your brain waves while torturing you with strobe lights.

"Where's my blankie? And do you mind if I suck my thumb?"

"Keep your eyes open, please." Flash. Flash. Flash. Directly into your eyes. Not exactly the disco scene you remember. More like how you imagine they must brainwash people who are in prisoner-of-war camps.

After the light show, you're ordered to go to sleep. You just experienced a laser show a few inches from your face, and now you're lying down in a closet with a stranger watching you sleep. How relaxed can you get? Just press the sleep button on one of those electrodes.

"God, this is weird. What brainiac developed this test? Those poor mice!"

You relax and try to be diligent. You want to do everything right. You want to prove you're seizureless when they take you off this stuff. You try to put your mind somewhere peaceful. You think of Narrow River in Narragansett, Rhode Island. You also try deep-breathing exercises, which you never mastered even during labor.

Your eyes are closed. The technician flashes the lights intermittently to monitor your brain waves.

Somehow you enter a light state of sleep.

JUST AS YOU HAD SUSPECTED, you don't have any activity or evidence of a past seizure. It's almost like the stroke was caused by an outside source.

Dr. Neuro is pleased with the test results. But he warns you that the fact that the results came back negative doesn't guarantee that seizure can't happen. You have still suffered a severe assault to your brain, a major bleed, surgery, and last but not least, a hole in your brain where a very large amount of blood was evacuated.

You smile and tell the neurologist, "Let's face it, I need another seizure like I need a hole in the head."

Silence.

"See, that's a joke. I *already* have a hole in the head."

"Ah," he says. "I see. Would you mind telling me ahead of time when the punch lines are coming? Might be easier for both of us."

"Sure. No problem."

He walks over and hugs you.

You hug back. Dr. Neuro has become part of the family, so it doesn't feel strange when you tell him that you love him.

What Goes Up . . .

YOU ARE DETERMINED to practice walking in your own house.

Which means you fall.

One day Jim is vacuuming upstairs and you crash down the stairs, landing in the entryway among the scattered rugs; now your limbs are scattered as well. You can't get up. When he stops vacuuming and looks down the stairs, he sees your feet. He freaks, as you knew he would.

This is how stroke affects the radius of the injured one—not just the afflicted person, but the family, the extended family, and the friends. In a way, everybody around you falls when you fall.

THE GARAGE IS a big source of falls. Eventually, you manage to fall both up and down the stairs that lead to the garage. It must be the way the steps are constructed, with a half step from the laundry to the garage-step landing.

One day, you step down carefully to put some paper in the recycle bin in the garage. Your ankle turns, things spread apart, and you realize that you are falling, very slowly, à la Alice in Wonderland. Alice fell continuously through the rabbit hole; you fall continuously, at every conceivable juncture of your own home.

It's surreal. Your legs are running away from home. You can do nothing to stop them.

When you "land," you are spread-eagled, one leg in the garage and the other leg in the laundry room. It's a complete split, with the doorjamb pressed up against your crotch. Nadia Comaneci couldn't get out of this position. But you don't call Jim.

It takes you almost a half hour to unwedge yourself. You feel like a parked car, with two cars sandwiching each bumper. As though you were a car getting out of such a spot, you do a fifty-three-point turn, inch by inch. By the time you free yourself from the door-jamb, you are sweating—but relieved that you don't have to put Jim through the trauma of finding you grimacing in the cheerleader position.

THERE ARE MANY falls in the bathroom. Once, feeling spunky, you try standing up in the shower on your own. Without using the shower chair, without anyone else in the room for support. You're feeling lucky—you want to feel normal again. People who have had strokes do give themselves showers. They do.

At first, it works. Your hair feels good—there's shampoo in it—and your body feels slippery. The water is hot. You lose track of time. Then you notice the tub rim hurtling toward you.

Your guardian angels take care of you, though, because you miss banging your head on the corner of a metal table by a few inches, hitting only the side of the tub with your neck. You're sprawled over the side. Everything has stopped but the water.

You feel your body when the shock wears off, and you definitely haven't broken any bones. But you have a hellacious time getting up. Water and bubbles everywhere.

You don't call Jim.

He would freak, and you're not too crazy about letting him see you as a human mop, washing the floor with the front half of your body, naked, with suds all over you. It might take him a while to get past that picture.

Half an hour later, using the shower chair as your anchor, you are back on your feet. The bathroom looks like a lake. You check the mirror; you look like a beached whale. It's a mess, but one thing is certain: You're clean as a whistle.

YOU TRY THE SAME shower maneuver the next day.

You get the same result.

Actually, you don't get *exactly* the same result. This time you shoot out of the tub as if someone had thrown you across the room and land all the way on the floor. You pick up quite a bit of momentum.

You are completely wedged up against the door, in the corner of the bathroom. It is so slippery that you have no chance whatsoever of getting up.

It's no use.

You have to call for help.

As you lie there, you recall a Valentine's Day card Jim made for you; it read, "Julia, A to Z." V was voluptuous; P was pilose, a soft covering of hair, referring to a Latin man at work who used to stroke your arm and say, "I love your hair." You had to get a dictionary and look up some of the silly love words he used: Z was for zaftig, meaning Rubenesque.

Maybe those letters would have different words attached to them now.

JIM HAS BEEN BATHING Rory in his bathroom; you don't want to alarm either one of them, so you try to keep your tone light: "Honey, I need your help for a second."

When he hears you, Jim rushes to the door. He's terrified, and you know it.

He can't open the door—it's unlocked, but your voluptuous zaftig body is blocking it like a dead bolt.

"I'm fine, I'm fine I'm fine I'm fine."

You can tell he is panicking; you keep trying to explain that you are okay, you just can't get up. He starts pushing the door with all his strength. You slide enough for him to squeeze through.

Your legs are up the wall. Bubbles are everywhere. You look like you're posing for *Playboy*. Sexy sexy.

You laugh.

Jim's not laughing though. To him, you are still a disaster in the corner, possibly injured. He stares at you. His face is white with panic.

"Okay," he gasps, "what do I do?"

"Hey, there," you say, with a provocative wink. "I've been waiting for you all of my life. Don't you want to jump my bones?"

Not Exactly the Therapy
You Had in Mind

YOU ARE SITTING at your desk. The computer screen is glowing. The cursor is blinking. Nothing is happening.

You had been thinking that you would be able to get employment somewhere down the road, but you realize, after an hour at the desk, that you simply no longer have the mental tools to put a portfolio or resumé together. You can no longer organize. You can no longer multitask. You can do one thing at a time, and you can only do that if you are paying very, very close attention. The policies and procedures you wrote before your stroke were, you realize, really composed by someone else. Someone you used to be.

This, the doctors tell you, is a result of the stroke. It's what happens when you have a brain deficit. Your ability to put things in sequence, and then handle them as they need to be dealt with—that sense of organization—has been lost with your stroke. That part of your brain has basically been blown to pieces. This is a big part of the reason you're regularly overwhelmed by fatigue from basic personal tasks like getting dressed.

Your days of being on the phone with a customer, working at your computer, and listening to one of the support reps at the door, all at the same time, are over.

You stare at the computer, at the empty screen and the blinking cursor waiting for you to take action.

You switch it off.

RORY THROWS a ball to you.

You are trying to get your left hand to work, trying to develop hand-eye coordination again. You watch the ball as it rolls on the floor to your son and try to pick it up in midair as he tosses it back. You want to make the left side work, and you want to include Rory.

He tosses.

You drop it.

He picks it up.

You roll it back.

He tosses.

You drop it.

He picks it up.

You roll it back.

Rory likes the game.

YOU HAVE DEVELOPED all kinds of little projects to improve yourself. You want to increase the strength in your hamstrings, which are very weak. You are leaning forward on a chair and Rory is behind you, lifting your leg up patiently, helping you improve your resilience.

"A little higher."

He lifts it higher.

"Okay, higher."

He pushes your leg up over his head—and then he drops it.

There's no time. You have no control. It's just like an anchor; it smashes into the tile floor with your toe pointing straight down. You fall to the floor. The pain is excruciating, and even with Rory there, you can't help letting out a little howl.

The toe, you realize, must be broken.

Rory is crying.

You can't even speak, it hurts so much. Your left side is hypersensitive to pain.

Jim rushes in. He heard the noise.

You think, *It's going to stop—the pain will stop—and then Jim is going to help me get up—and then I'm going to get this hamstring strong again—and I'm going to walk like I used to.*

Rory is still crying. Jim is comforting him while pulling you up from the floor. At least somebody can still do two things at once.

Maybe lifting your leg isn't Rory's job.

Dealing with What You Have

ONE PARTICULAR OUTPATIENT THERAPIST at the center never seems to click with you.

The two of you don't manage to establish good chemistry, and you realize now how important that is for people who suddenly find themselves in a relationship with a therapist. One person might be great for person A but not for person B, and you find with this therapist that he must have assumed that you were in la-la land because you always talked about getting better.

His attitude—like that of so many of the caregivers you have inherited—is basically, "Well, you just have to learn to deal with what you have." Maybe there are some patients who need that kind of approach in order to figure out how to deal with their situation. But there are other patients—you, for instance—who are willing to fight, willing to step out of the box and not set the ceiling for themselves.

"You know," you told him yesterday, "if I took the attitude you're recommending—'Learn to live with what's left'—I'd still be in a wheelchair, drooling. I'm going to Rollerblade with my son."

He says, "Yeah, well, there are ceilings in this life after something like a stroke happens to you."

■ ■ ■

THIS MORNING, you actually say to him, "My ceiling is only blue skies. When I look up to the sky I know that I have so much more improving to do. I'm a work in progress, as everybody is, and I'm not going to give up."

He looks at you over the top of his glasses and says, "Okay, I respect that, but what, specifically, does it mean?"

"It means I am disappointed with my gait. I find myself staring at people walking, trying to relearn the mechanics. I really feel labored when I'm walking, and I want to get that heel-toe action going, but my toes don't work. It means my heels really don't work either, which is weird because, I mean, what do you need your heels for? That's what I thought before all this. Well, you need your heels to strike the ground and then you press off with your toe. Mine don't work. Also your heel is very handy for keeping you stabilized and balanced, and because mine is impaired, I have balance blind spots. My heel on my left side has caused more backward falls for me. I have a lot of backward falls because of my heel not having the proper sensation or strength."

He nods a little.

"It means I'm not done yet," you continue. "In fact, I'm not done getting better until I'm in my grave. My epitaph may say 'Okay, I'm done.' Please don't act like you're done with me. We need to work on my gait."

He nods a little again, the same way.

THE TWO OF YOU work on your gait, but you can tell that he is getting frustrated.

He has broken your gait down to four components. It's not that you don't understand his instruction. Your left side simply won't listen to your brain's instructions.

Therapists have certain measurements, and one of them is for the Achilles tendon. Yours are very, very stiff on both sides, and that is related to two things. Some of it is due to the stroke, but most of it is related to a surgery you had on both your heels back in 1990 and 1991 that moved your Achilles tendon to remove some golf-ball-size bone spurs. That contributed to the tightness in your heels. So your foot movement is limited, and when he measures, there isn't much improvement.

You ask, "What do I need to do?"

He sighs.

BACK AT THE HOUSE, on your own, you hang off the steps from your toes, holding on to the railing and just letting your heels stretch that way. The tightness is intense. It almost feels like your heels are tearing away.

But when you check your heel range, it has improved—the tiniest bit, but it has improved.

Bitter Prescription

YOU RELUCTANTLY CONSENT to more chemotherapy. Dr. Jerk is hammering his diagnosis and treatment to your neurologist. Dr. Neuro is still working on a diagnosis, getting facts and dismissing possibilities via testing. Being unclear of causation, he diplomatically states that he can't rule out Dr. Jerk's treatment and suggests that you consider following it until he has more conclusive information.

Dr. Jerk writes the prescription for a high dosage of the chemotherapy drug, Cytoxan, potassium (to ensure hydration), and Mesna (an antinausea drug).

YOU WILL BE AN OUTPATIENT for the day. It will be a ten-hour session. Then you can go home for a while.

The outpatient infusion room is a dismal, depressing place. The atmosphere is austere, and the reasons people are there never make one feel optimistic. You need a total blood count prior to the infusion. You have to wait over an hour for the blood work results. You have lots of company.

You envision a skull and crossbones right on the bag. You have to go to the bathroom constantly because of the hydration. You have to do it right there next to the bed. You have to wait for the nurse to help you struggle off the bed and onto the little potty; meanwhile you have another patient right next to you on the other side of this thin veil of a curtain. Everybody in the room can hear exactly what you are doing. You do what you have to do.

Why is it that the curtain supposedly used to create privacy only causes more interest in what's going on behind it?

The curtain doesn't close completely; there's a wide gap at the ends. There was a time when that would have bothered you. But once you have been in the hospital and had enough things done to you, you learn to just stare at the curtain and pee.

Potted

FURTHER ALONG in your recovery now. You are obviously making more progress, because you go out for social occasions—*without* the leg brace that has become standard equipment for you during walking lessons.

You are at your house again, feeling somewhat normal . . . wearing shoes, even. You are dressed to go out with friends. Jim is upstairs getting ready. You are standing in the kitchen waiting. But you have blind spots that affect your balance; if you start to fall a certain way, there is no way you can catch yourself. There is simply no safety net; your left heel doesn't work, nor do any of the toes on your left foot.

Winnie, your cat, pounces in front of you, causing you to reel backward. There is no hope of sparing the fall. You plunge backward, making a tremendous noise, as usual. Falling is less scary now than it was, though.

You're not moving. Actually, you are sitting. You have executed a perfect butt plant ("plant" being the operative word). You're sitting smack in the middle of a large potted hydrangea in the corner of the room, dirt smeared along the back of your nice outfit. Broken branches and leaves are everywhere. Jim materializes, panting for breath. He must have skipped every step coming down the stairs. "I thought the kitchen was falling into the basement."

"Honey," you say, "I've been potted, my soil's a little dry, can you grab the watering can?"

A Walker Disguised
as a Stroller

JIM BUYS YOU a jogging stroller.

The idea is for Rory to sit in the stroller while you walk. This serves two purposes—first, you will be getting exercise, and second, you will have some stability as you move. Instead of using a walker, you'll have the stroller, and be able to cover a lot more ground and get a bigger feeling of accomplishment.

It's one of those heavy-duty strollers that holds up to eighty pounds. In the beginning Rory doesn't mind riding in it, but as time goes on you have to bribe him: "I will do this for you if you do this for me."

YOU'RE OUT SHOPPING with Jim and Rory. At the store you're visiting, there's a little movie and a video with a bench so the kids can watch movies while the parents are shopping. There are about eight kids around the TV. You are kind of hovering behind the scenes, and you hear one of the kids say, "What happened to your mother?"

"Well . . ."

You can see that he is trying to speak in low tones, probably because he doesn't want to hurt your feelings. You look away and pretend you can't hear anything, pretend you're going about your business, but you really make a point of listening to his answer.

"Well . . . ," he goes on, "she had an emergency and had to go to the hospital, and it broke her leg."

This is how he has processed your injury. The other boy asks something else, but you can't make it out, and Rory's response is even quieter. Maybe he doesn't want to draw attention to you, maybe he doesn't want to draw attention to himself, but you know he's trying to protect your feelings.

He is always so compassionate, so concerned about how you feel.

Moving On

YOU ARE NOW USING the stroller every night. Rory helps you to work out by taking his seat. You move around the neighborhood together, night after night, week after week.

Then one day it dawns on you.

Thanks to all the nights with Rory and the stroller, thanks to the many grueling months of rehab, thanks to the seemingly endless series of pool sessions and walking lessons, both with therapists and on your own initiative—you're now walking more or less independently around your house.

Under your own power.

Up and down the stairs.

When you want.

You are not walking *exactly* as you walked before the stroke, but you *are* walking. If you had listened to the people who told you solemnly that you would be in a wheelchair for the rest of your life— and that your failing to accept this was "denial"—what a different life you would be leading.

If it is a determined mind that springs recovery, that's definitely what you have.

■ ■ ■

YOU WANT TO PROVE something to yourself—and to Berbie. A walk-athon for the Jimmy Fund charity is taking place in Boston, and you want to be part of it. There is a contingent that is walking the whole twenty-six miles, and then there is another contingent that is doing half that, thirteen miles. Finally, there is the three-mile walk, which is what you have signed up Jim, Rory, and yourself to do. Berbie and her husband had set up Team Daisy to raise money for the Jimmy Fund. The team had grown each year, with many families and friends wanting to help a cause that benefits so many children with cancer.

You want to complete the three miles for the Jimmy Fund. You want to be part of the Team Daisy contingent. It's important to you to show your support and prove to yourself that you can contribute. It's a huge undertaking, because up to this point you really have not walked any significant distance. Three miles is a lot for someone who has had a stroke and is still partially paralyzed.

In preparation for the walk, you have been pushing yourself, in your brace, to increase your stamina. You can walk a mile or so with the jogging stroller that Jim gave you for Mother's Day, but a mile and a half is murder, and it takes you a very long time, sometimes as much as two hours, depending on the kind of day you're having. You can never be sure what kind of day you're going to have after a stroke; one day you can feel great and the next you can feel lousy.

For a while, you think it is the weather that makes everything hurt so much when you train for the walk, but then you conclude that there is simply no rhyme or reason to your body's reactions. Some days you are in more pain and are more exhausted than others. There's chronic pain and you have to put it in the background. If you bring it to the foreground, it can take over your day and your life.

That, you decide, is not going to happen. As you prepare for the walk, you're constantly putting pain in the backseat. You may have had a stroke, but the stroke is not going to have you.

Time to complete the three miles for the Jimmy Fund, for Daisy, and for yourself. Time to move on with your life.

Limping for Joy

RORY DOES NOT WANT to ride in the stroller on the Jimmy Fund walk. You have to draft your godson, Olly, Berbie's older boy, who is about sixty pounds, to sit in the stroller. It's better to have more weight in the stroller. You feel like you have more stability, and you get to work out your arms at the same time.

They are long, very long miles, but you finish all three of them with Jim by your side. It takes you more than three hours, and there's a lot of pain, and you're more tired than you can ever remember being in your life by the time you finish. But you do it.

You are extremely proud of yourself. But as Jim drives you home you wonder whether you're going to be laid up for a while.

THE WALK SETS YOU BACK so badly that you are out of action for two weeks. You miss some of your therapies because the spasticity really kicks up after such extensive activity.

You realize that you've overdone it. It's tough. But you tell Jim that it was worth every step to have achieved it.

Your Own Problems

SUNSET. You are sitting in your headquarters chair staring at the shadows on the wall, feeling depressed, drooling quite a bit, and you do not have much control over it. Your face is flaccid; the muscle control is so weak it just sags.

Jim wants to talk about work and you are too tired. You have started to realize that it is unlikely you will ever go back to work.

You have been looking for ways to avoid accepting that, thinking of ways that you could do it, but having only the right side makes it difficult. You know there are adaptive devices, but knowing you don't have the energy level that it takes to be in a fast-paced work environment has set you into a funk.

You can't work.

You also feel you are failing as a stay-at-home mom. Rory needs a lot of motherly care, and you're not able to do it, since you cannot even care for yourself. You have to rely on your mother and Jim as the primary caretakers for Rory.

Rory does not understand the magnitude of what has happened, really, but he senses that something is very different. He knows that you are injured and that something important has changed. When you were in the hospital he would get frustrated; he would want to go home, he would want you to be home. You were gone for a couple of months and he had been shuffled around a lot—to your mother, to Jim, and to friends who covered when neither of them was available.

Rory realizes that you always need someone at home to baby-sit *you*. You need someone to help you with your needs. He has stopped going to you for anything *he* needs.

MIDNIGHT. You're in bed. A call from Rory's room. He is not feeling well.

You say to Jim, "Please let me go try and console him."

You go into Rory's room. He says, "I want Daddy, I don't want you."

He says it over and over again. He's emphatic about it.

You say, "Well, let Mommy help you," and he says, "No, you can't help me. You have your own problems. You fall down and you need help and you need someone to get you up."

You go back to your bedroom. Jim takes care of Rory.

You don't get to sleep for a long time.

A Trip to the Bahamas

FOR THE CHEMOTHERAPY infusions you have agreed to, you choose to have your blood work done the day before, thus sparing you several boring hours in the waiting room while they process the results. Sometimes you go for blood work on a Sunday at the sister hospital near your home. Often the phlebotomist tells you that it's "not ordered for Sunday," which causes another long wait for your approval to churn its way through the hospital's computer system.

You'd think someone on the medical staff would give you a heads-up. But you really do have to figure this stuff out for yourself. For instance, you learn that you always want to be the first patient to arrive in the infusion room. This gives you a selection of where you will be planted for the day. The room has strategically placed beds and lounge chairs; you learn to think about location. Do you want to be near the TV, near the restrooms, or near the entrance where there's human activity to observe? You opt for the bed because you are still having problems with balance and the sitting position hurts your leg; fluid pools up. You want the one near the entrance because you can watch television and also see new faces entering the room.

There's only one nurse attending to all the patients in the in-fusion room. You learn that it's best to endear yourself to her. If she doesn't like you, you tend to have a very bad day. If she decides that she wants to help you, as opposed to *having* to help you because it's her job, the day goes much more smoothly. You realize that she's seen human suffering every day for a long time, and has had to create a hardened shell in order to survive.

Knowing that you are going to be there for an extended stay, you let Jim equip your little bag with "keeping busy" items. He bought you a Walkman, which goes in the bag; you bring books on tape and a tablet if you want to write or sketch. Most of the time, you just sit and observe the workings of the room—the people coming, the people going—and think about what the other people who are hooked up to needles and bags are there for.

It's a long day.

ANOTHER DAY OF INFUSION. You are all settled in and the IV is going. Jim has left to go to work. You think it is going to be the latest in a sequence of boring days. You know what the next week will bring—a hangover without the party.

But you're wrong. It's not like the last time.

Jim has e-mailed all your friends, alerting them to the fact that you are being infused; they show up on a prearranged sched-ule. People keep materializing. Everyone takes an hour and comes and sits with you. So most of the day, you are simply being enter-tained. It's a wonderful surprise.

AT THE END OF THE DAY, you are finishing up, and you are waiting for Jim to pick you up. A short man with patches of reddish hair and a really bad comb-over, who has been hooked up to his IV for almost as long as you have, has been watching you hold court the whole time. Now all your friends are gone, all the other patients have left, and it's just you and Mr. Comb-Over.

You turn and smile at him, sharing the pleasant, anticipated moment of being done, finally, with the day's treatment. But his round face is scarlet with rage.

"Oh, I'm glad to see something's wrong with you," he hisses. "The way you acted all day, you would have thought you were here on vacation in the Bahamas."

He is angry with you for finding something other than unhappiness and rage at this situation.

You have spent the day laughing with your friends, but that is how you diverted your attention from your problems. You made light of things, sure, but you always made light of yourself, not of anyone else. You cracked good jokes about your situation. You stayed sane because you allowed yourself to laugh. Now this person is angry that you were laughing—not at anything in particular that you were laughing about, but at *the fact of your laughter.*

You look right at him and say, "I bet that really pissed you off that I was laughing."

"Yes," he mutters, "it did."

"Well," you ask, "what do you have?"

"I have colon cancer."

"I'm sorry to hear that."

His face is still red. He stares at you and says, "This hospital did it to me."

You think about this for a minute, and say, "No one did anything to anybody here. We are here because this is what we have to go through. You know, with your attitude, you are going to die."

Silence.

"Your *attitude,*" you continue, "is what is going to get you through this, and if you have an attitude that is negative and blaming, then you will not have any energy left to put toward your recovery."

You keep talking. He starts to listen to you only after he finds out what has happened to you. You don't volunteer it. He finally asks you, and you tell him that you have had a massive brain hemorrhage that has resulted in left-side paralysis, and that they are still trying to diagnose it, but they felt that the chemotherapy was at least a cautionary treatment.

He's shocked. He says, "You're younger than my youngest daughter. I have four daughters, and you are younger than my youngest daughter."

This seems to make him able to see the human side of the situation. You keep talking. He is now listening intently to you talk about changing his attitude and being more positive about recovery. He nods and even smiles a little.

His wife and daughter come over and hug and kiss you and say, "Thank you so much. This is the first time in almost eight months he's changed his mood. He just needed somebody who was going through something as serious as he was."

"Positive thought," you say, "is all you have. Remind him when he needs a boost."

They promise they will. They leave.

Over the Edge

LAST OF THE CHEMOTHERAPY TRIPS. Thank God.

You opt for a chair beside a man who is there having some type of strong antibiotic or superdrug to kill the infection raging through his body. His wife is there. You can see how upset and worried she is, and she fusses around him all day. He has obviously lost a lot of weight; he's gaunt and an odd color of gray, very sick. You sense he's not going to make it, and pray that you're wrong.

It's a very sad room.

There are a lot of stories within these walls. Some of them are victorious, some of them aren't. You think again about the things you said to calm down the guy who was mad at your laughing. Not laughing today. Just trying to get to the end of the session.

You reach into your bag for your prenatal vitamins and swallow them with the cup of water Jim has left for you. You can't wait to see him again—he's your rock.

All in all, you really do hate coming here. The ride to the hospital is always somber. You fight back tears sometimes to spare Jim. Maybe Mr. Comb-Over had a point. You know what's ahead for the next ten hours, and it sucks. Whenever you weep here, which does happen, you try to keep quiet.

■ ■ ■

AT THE END OF THE DAY you say a prayer of thanks, because you've finished all of the precautionary treatments.

Before you leave, you follow up with Dr. Jerk. He feels you need another treatment. Dr. Neuro concurs, because he's still trying to figure out the cause. So it's all been a mistake. You have to go back again next month for another treatment and you have to sign something and you can't see what the nurse wants you to sign.

You lose it.

You have been happy and jovial through all the appointments, right up to today, when the finish line is in sight, but this time, at the end of the appointment, the nurse tells you the plan has been changed, and you completely lose it.

It's like being told you're uncured. Like being told you have to go back to hell. You have been robbed of completion. The finish line has been moved ahead. And everything you're feeling feels worse because of the intravenous poisoning you've just had to endure.

You feel lied to. Anything anyone says isn't real. Anything that sounds like a statement is really a question.

It's not fair.

Who decides what's fair, anyway?

You hear yourself screaming, like somebody else is actually doing it.

You hear yourself yelling profanities, telling her that you are sick of this shit and that you don't want to do it anymore.

It really surprises Dr. Neuro, because you haven't done that at all through the whole process of your injury. He's completely taken aback.

Jim has materialized somehow. He calms you down, but it's tough. He brings you downstairs to the coffee room. You hear yourself crying and crying, saying over and over again that you don't want to do it—you simply can't do it again. People are staring. You don't give a damn. Let them stare, it doesn't change anything.

You hear yourself, as if from a great distance:

Had it.

Had it up to here with the fucking medical community.

Only one goddamned thing I want from you bastards in your white smocks and that is to be *left alone.*

Jim fixes your gaze and says, "Don't you want to pull yourself together? This is the day when you were going to make your trip to the office."

Your friends at work.

You'd completely blanked that this was your day to go back.

He always remembers these things.

"I don't *want* to go."

Like an exhausted child having a temper tantrum. That shrill, that desperate.

The Blockhead Club

YOU DO NOT, IN FACT, want to go back to the office. But Jim has convinced you that you must pull yourself together, because they are all expecting you there for a little visit. So you do.

The silent drive to your office. Pulling yourself together.

As Jim drives, the roads go by like nothing happened and you are just late for work.

YOU ARE NOW HOBBLING through cubicles that seem both familiar and part of another dimension, part of an arrangement in space that must have been invented for someone else.

One of your coworkers shows you "your" new office space. They've tried to decorate it as you would. But you've never been there. It's a stranger's office.

You don't belong here anymore. You recognize the faces, but you realize that you will probably never, ever belong here again.

You put on a happy face, you don't let anyone know what is wrong or tell them that you will have to do more chemotherapy. They are nervous and tentative around you, in part because of what happened, and in part because you simply don't look the way you looked the last time you were there. You are on industrial-strength doses of steroids as well as a cocktail of other drugs, and your face is swollen and misshapen, like a pumpkin head. The skin is very taut and puffy and seems like someone else's skin. The drugs literally make your face hurt; it hurts to smile, but you do it anyway.

Smiling should never hurt.

YOU TAKE A BREAK and Jim escorts you to the women's room.

You stare into the mirror. Your eyes are little slits from the swelling; your cropped dark hair frames your face. The steroids also mess up your hairline, pulling it down oddly. It now extends to your cheeks and chin. You're a great candidate for an exhibit at the circus: the bearded lady.

It's a rectangular face now. You have literally become a blockhead.

You splash some water on your face and make your way out to see Jim.

"I'M STARTING A CLUB," you say.

"That's good. What's it called?"

"The Blockhead Club."

You decide to draft members with the same facial structure. Janet Reno, for instance. She doesn't know it, but she's the president of the club. She can keep all the blockheads in order. Jimmy Johnson, ex-coach of the Miami Dolphins, is included too; his hair and angular face might even get him into the Blockhead Hall of Fame.

Looking around the office, you and Jim launch the first blockhead alert. Before long, you both instantly know who has just, unknowingly, joined the club.

You laugh.

Thank God.

THE DRIVE BACK HOME. The roads go by like nothing happened, and Jim is just taking you back home from work.

You say, "I'm not going to be on chemotherapy for the rest of my life, like Dr. Jerk recommends."

Silence.

You say, "We're getting a second opinion."

"You're Incurable."
"I Want a Second Opinion."
"Okay, You're Also a
Pain in the Ass."

YOU GET THE FEELING people at the hospital don't really want you to get a second opinion from outside their system.

They put up a major fuss about transferring your (huge) file, and tell you there are plenty of doctors within the hospital who can review your case.

You don't want a doctor from within the hospital.

Dr. Jerk, in particular, is uneasy about the whole undertaking, but when you insist, he authorizes a referral and tells you that you can send your records to a specialist at another hospital. The records are quite extensive at this point—they're like a manuscript for one of those long historical romance sagas, and a good deal more difficult to get through. But you send them anyway, and set up an appointment with the other specialist to review them. You make sure that the records arrive early, leaving the doctor plenty of time to become familiar with your case.

■ ■ ■

THE HOSPITAL IS over an hour away by car. Jim is taking time off from work to drive you.

You arrive early, which is good, because you have to go through the whole process of being registered in admitting, and getting a hospital medical card, for your one-time visit. That chews up another hour.

In the doctor's office, you and Jim wait.

Your records are sitting there on his desk, and you're tempted to start reviewing them yourself to make sure you're every bit as familiar with them as the new doctor will be when he arrives to see what secret notes doctors write but don't share with you. You're reminded of the *Seinfeld* episode where Elaine goes crazy trying to find out what her therapist jots down on that pad.

But you don't peek.

WHEN THE DOCTOR, a trim, nervous-looking man with carefully combed auburn hair, finally arrives, you stand up and shake hands and say hello and sit down again and ask him what his initial take is on the records of your case.

And he says to you, "I haven't looked at them yet."

You close your eyes and take a deep breath to squelch your anger.

You and Jim are there solely for a second opinion based on your (now massive) medical file. Jim is missing work for this. You sent the records weeks ago. And the doctor knows absolutely nothing about you except that you have been referred to him.

Dr. Jerk the Second.

He's actually trying to "read" these hundreds of pages right in front of you, sifting and glancing through them. He is shuffling through the dozens of folders for the first time right now, and creating his "second opinion" for you on the spot. You are going to feel extremely confident with this man's thoughts on your well-being. Sure.

■ ■ ■

DR. JERK THE SECOND is younger than Dr. Jerk, and not, apparently, any more inclined to make waves than he is to read medical records. The safe option is to agree with Dr. Jerk's treatment plan. And that is exactly what he does, without even so much as a physical evaluation. Yes, chemotherapy will be necessary for the rest of your life.

He's done. But you're not.

"Well," you say, "my first opinion of *you* is that you're arrogant. And my second opinion is that you're a jerk. Thanks for absolutely nothing. I hope you still have enough of a conscience to realize that we shouldn't be charged for this nonvisit, or for your nonopinion. But you may already be a complete zombie, like some of these other doctors, so I'm not placing any bets on your conscience actually existing anymore."

End of meeting.

YOU AND YOUR HUSBAND have driven far beyond your home and worked your way through the alleys of another hospital in the hope of receiving objective advice from a doctor who did not know Dr. Jerk. In fact, you realize, every doctor "knows" every other doctor—through consults, conferences, and studies. They simply stick with each other's diagnosis. It doesn't matter what specialist you consult. You will never get an original opinion, because they will be basing their opinion on the original specialist's notes. And when is one specialist going to challenge the opinion of another one?

Walking to the parking lot, you say to Jim, "I'm pissed. What a total waste of time."

He nods.

He unlocks the car doors. He helps you into your seat. He walks around the car and settles in behind the wheel.

You both sit there completely dumbfounded that another human being could casually condemn you to chemotherapy poisoning for the rest of your life.

You say, "I don't need the chemotherapy. Most likely I never needed it."

He stares out the windshield toward the expressway.

"Whatever happened to my brain happened because of something I did before I had the hemorrhage. My intuition tells me that. I am absolutely certain of it, Jim. Once we get rid of whatever it was that caused the hemorrhage, we can let time heal my wound."

He nods a little tiny nod and starts the car. He's scared.

DR. NEURO SAYS he's not sure he agrees with Dr. Jerk and that he would like you to see the expert on strokes.

"Dr. Renown," he tells you calmly, "is so much more knowledgeable than I am about strokes. He can give us some insight."

You can't believe he said that. Dr. Neuro has an M.D. and a Ph.D. in neurology, and he humbly says someone else is smarter than he is. Your best interests are what matters. He's not stuck in some diagnosis tug-of-war. He always speaks respectfully of the opinions of other doctors, but he honestly isn't sure about this diagnosis.

You love Dr. Neuro.

DR. RENOWN is an older man, with thinning white hair, and his wise, kind eyes beam out from behind little wire spectacles. He has a gentle manner. The first thing he asks is, "What do you think happened to you?"

Well, you like his approach so far.

You explain that you're here to see him because you are now scheduled for your fourth angiogram in six months and you've also been told you need to be on chemotherapy for life. Dr. Jerk's opinion is that without it, you will end up on a respirator and die an awful death.

You explain that your intuition is telling you that you'll have another stroke if you go through another angiogram—you just know your body couldn't tolerate it. You also need an opinion on the chemotherapy, because you don't feel it's what you need. You feel you need time to heal, that's all.

You tell him about Daisy, and about the drugs they wanted to put her on, drugs that would probably have killed her. How you knew the doctors were wrong then. And how you know Dr. Jerk is wrong now.

After listening, Dr. Renown puts your films up on the lighted board and shows you the progression of your healing. Then he says something that makes your heart glow.

"What happened to you was from an outside source. It wasn't anything that was wrong with your brain or your body. I think you should keep listening to your intuition. It's been correct all along."

Then you ask the question that's been waiting patiently for its turn.

"Nobody in the medical community—no doctor, no nurse, not even Dr. Neuro—has been willing to tell me flat out that I'm not going to die from this. My family has told me I'm not going to die, but no one with a white coat, not yet. Am I going to make it?"

He takes off his spectacles and polishes them with a cloth, using the opportunity to look you directly in the eye with no barrier. "You will have deficits for the rest of your life," he says. "Your arm and hand will be impaired and your left side will continue to be a problem in general, but you're not going to die. Your films show that your brain has already healed. Go, live your life."

On the way home, you're the happiest you have felt in a long, long time.

In the Mood

YOU AND JIM have not made love for nearly a year after your injury, a long time to be apart. So much has happened in between, emotionally and physically. You no longer feel like the same person Jim married; you feel more like half a person; half of your body just doesn't exist in your mind. You feel crippled.

If he could have seen the future in a glass ball, wouldn't he have run as fast as he could away from the altar? This isn't what he bargained for. You have aged way beyond your years; some days you feel as though you've been sent at warp speed to an age of seventy without the benefit of all the memories in between.

You are both fearful of making love because you have had a tremendous assault to your vascular system. Jim is literally afraid he is going to kill you. Having an orgasm would cause your blood pressure to rise, and who could say that wouldn't bring on another stroke? You're scared, too.

What a way to go, though. At least Jim could have the legacy of having killer sex.

But the doctors had said intercourse is now okay, and on this point, for some reason, you are finally inclined to take their word on something.

■ ■ ■

YOU'RE APPREHENSIVE because your body is not operating the way it had prior to your injury. If you can't see your left side, it doesn't exist—you can't feel it. You have to be looking at your left side to know where it is in space. At night when you go to bed, Jim would hold your hand under the covers. Initially, you'd feel the warmth of his hand and the pressure, but within minutes that message would go away and you wouldn't know he was holding your hand anymore. You'd feel pinned down and you wouldn't know why. How's that for a mood enhancer? "Hey, do you have my hand? What are you doing with it? Where is it? When you're done with it, I want it back."

So you have your little black humor about the body parts.

You discover quickly that you aren't able to participate in the lovemaking the way you used to. You're numb. Adjusting to the numbness of the whole left side of your face and body does not, at first, feel very sensual. Imagine having sex with the whole left side of your body on novocaine. Your leg is basically a Jersey barrier—dead weight. You can't move the way you used to, and it doesn't feel the same. The left side of your face lacks any muscle tone, which causes you to drool profusely, and although Jim has dealt with every body fluid possible, you're grossed out for him. It certainly didn't make you feel sexy or appealing. "Julia, it's nothing new, you've always drooled over me," Jim says lightly after sensing your reticence.

But Jim thoughtfully leaves the light on so you can see your left side. He helps to move you. He does a lot of weight lifting, but he is sweet and devoted. It occurs to you that he has been making love to you tirelessly, in a nonphysical sense, from the moment you were injured. He has taken care of your every need, and always in a loving manner.

Now is no different.

■ ■ ■

WHEN YOU ARE DONE, you both cry a little and hold each other.

"Now we're a couple again," Jim whispers.

He's been a nurse for so long. It is a huge relief to both of you that you've passed the caretaker barrier together, that you're back to the intimacy a husband and wife are meant to share.

Slip-Sliding Away

WINTER IS TOUGH. It makes your muscle tone and spasticity problems really kick in. You find that you take more long naps in the winter than in summer. You've become a classic study in hibernation.

IT'S A GRAY AFTERNOON in February. You aren't feeling well. It's sleeting outside and everything is coated with ice and pouring rain.

Although the bus stop is only a block away, you don't want to have to walk to meet the bus in this miserable weather, so you hop in the car to pick Rory up. You don't bother to put your coat on, and you're still in your slippers.

You collect Rory without incident, and he's very glad to see you. Once he is buckled in, you head back down the street and decide to pick up the mail from your mailbox.

You know you can't walk down the driveway in this weather, so you pull the car as close to the box as possible. There is a mound of plowed snow by the curb, though, so you aren't able to get close enough to grab the mail from the window. You open the car door and step out.

Big mistake.

You slide on a slab of ice that is covered with a pool of water. Under the idling car you go.

You're flat on your back, and you quickly realize you can't get up on your own.

The car is rumbling above you, and you're lying on a dark, frigid bed of ice and water. You can hear that Rory is agitated. He is calling for you.

He is trying to open the door, and every time he does this he hits your head. You keep saying, "Rory, stop that," and you know he's starting to panic a little bit.

He gets out the other door and makes his way around to where you are. He hears the car running and sees you under the car. It's a scary thing for him. It's no picnic for you, either. You have no idea how you are going to get yourself out of this ugly situation.

Fortunately, you see your neighbor Charlie step out of his front door with his little girl and start toward his car. Thank God, he has to drive his daughter somewhere. He's a big, strapping guy, just what you need at the moment.

You call to him; he turns his head and looks puzzled.

He comes over and hoists you from underneath the car.

He says, "Julia, what are you doing?"

You say, "I just went out for a little ice-skating; I do this every once in a while. It's a new type of skating—you do it under your car. For a real adrenaline rush, the car should be running."

You're being a smart-ass. Then you notice Rory is still looking at you with eyes the size of saucers. "Actually, I was just trying to get my mail, but it turns out that's not a good idea when you're wearing slippers. No traction. Guess that's why they're called 'slippers.'"

He reaches over and gets your mail and hands it to you. He buckles Rory back in. Soaked from head to toe, you get in your car and drive the six feet up the driveway and into the dry warmth of the garage.

You Must Be So Proud

"WHEN ARE YOU DUE?"

You get this question from strangers quite often.

"When am I due what? Oh, you thought I was pregnant. You must know something I don't know."

You can handle any amount of pain, and you have become numb to most forms of public humiliation, but when someone asks you when you are having your baby, it feels like you are staked in the heart.

The stroke caused hemiparesis, which means one side is affected and certain muscle groups either don't work or are extremely weak. You never had a washboard stomach, and some of the muscle groups in your abdomen and your hips are weak or don't work at all. You sometimes stand with your hips jutting out if you don't pay attention. If you're not doing a pelvic tilt and pulling your gut in consciously, which is difficult to do at a time in your life when *everything* has become a conscious task, including things like lifting your leg high enough that you don't fall when you walk, you'll have sloppy posture. So it does look like you have an extra ten pounds or so. You have thin legs and your weight tends to gravitate to the stomach area. The way you stand can appear to make you look pregnant.

But you can't take it when people assume that you are and start talking to you about it.

■ ■ ■

ONE WOMAN in a waiting room for one of your many doctor's visits asks you what happened; she notices the brace on your leg and your cane.

You explain you have had a stroke.

She pats your stomach and said, "Oh . . . it can't be that bad, at least you have a little one on the way."

"Actually, it's not a 'little one,' it's a big one that you just tactfully pointed out for the public at large. I'm not pregnant, but thank you for reminding me of my weight problem."

You can't understand why complete strangers feel they can take liberties with pregnant women by touching their stomachs. Would they grab a big-busted woman and say, "Just wanted to feel if they were real"?

YOU GO TO THE LOCAL PHARMACY to pick up your supply of prescriptions. This is during flu season and the pharmacy is crowded.

There is a new lady at the register, and as you're paying for your package, she says, "I sees you are about to have your baby."

Great. Not only do you look pregnant, you look nine months pregnant.

You just look at her and say, "The only thing I am about to deliver is fifty pounds of fat. I'm not going to have a baby."

This produces a pregnant pause.

Everyone is staring at your stomach; you try to suck it in with all your might. She is so flustered that she tries to give you more change from your transaction than you have coming.

AT THE GROCERY STORE, a huge woman guides her cart next to yours, grins broadly, and says, "My, you're getting big. You must be so excited!"

You smile right back and say, "What a big ass you have. You must be so proud!"

It felt good at the time. But later you feel a pang of guilt. Why are you so very sensitive about this issue?

End of Discussion

DR. NEURO has been keeping you on prenatal vitamins for a long time, supposedly on the theory that it is always a possibility that you will become pregnant again.

Today, during a checkup, he informs you that this was not necessary after all, and that he has prescribed the vitamins simply to keep your mental attitude positive.

"It's time for you to know," he says calmly, "that you really can't have a baby."

It's like a sock in the jaw, but for some reason you don't argue or contradict him, which you would certainly have done earlier on in your recovery.

"First and foremost, your body probably cannot handle the stress of becoming pregnant. Second, Jim has so much on his plate. Look at the whole picture for a minute, okay? The bottom line is that you very well might not survive the delivery—and you might not even survive the pregnancy itself. I know all that's probably hard for you to process. But think about Jim for a minute."

The sentence rolls around in your head for a minute. *Think about Jim.*

When you have mentioned to other people how committed

you are to having a baby, a lot of them have asked, "Well, how does your husband feel about this?" You've always said, "Jim is behind me one hundred percent." He always was, of course, but something tells you now, as the doctor says these words to you, that Jim has known for some time that this was a crazy idea, but has been unable to say that to you.

Then it dawns on you. Jim needed Dr. Neuro to tell you.

You respect your neurologist. He has been with you from the beginning, he has asked you questions instead of just issuing orders, and he knows who you were and what you are about. Jim knows all this. It was inconceivable that the neurologist would be talking this way to you without having talked to Jim about it first.

You let this new reality wash over you for a moment. The doctor's lips are moving, but you can't make out what he's saying.

There will be no new baby. It's a fact now.

YOU PICK THE NEUROLOGIST up in midsentence.

". . . you had a stroke and you became totally incapacitated. Then what?"

You shake your head briskly for just a second. You do want to be part of this conversation.

"What do you mean?" you ask.

"I mean, suppose, God forbid, you became even more seriously paralyzed, and suppose Jim was stuck with two children to take care of? And you? How fair would that be to him?"

Think about Jim.

He is putting it in terms that are not all about Julia, making you think about Jim, and not what your goals are.

He's right.

The having-a-baby part of your life is over.

You were always apprehensive when thinking of trying to care for a baby. When you tried to think it through, though, you knew you wouldn't even be able to hold a baby without putting it in harm's way. So you would just leave it that you were going to have another baby, but you couldn't think about what would happen after the baby was born.

It has always been an impossibility. It is something that you used to get you to where you are now, a form of self-protection. It was a goal that had a purpose, and supported you, but it was never going to be achieved—you couldn't take care of yourself on your own. It must have been *you* who needed to hear it from the man who was taking care of you medically.

"Let me ask you something," you say. "When you put me on those prenatal vitamins, did you do that so I would still have the goal of having another child. To keep me from interrupting my recovery."

There really aren't any question marks. You are asking questions, but stating them as facts.

"I had to treat the mind," Dr. Neuro says, "as well as the body."

So there will be no baby. It is a huge, cold, dark fact. But it is not really unfamiliar. It wells up inside your chest and says, *You knew the time that you'd be asking him about babies was coming.* And you realize you are weeping.

He gives you some privacy. You weep for about half an hour there in the examination room.

Something you have always wanted has been taken away from you, and it isn't fair. You are devastated by this news, and it is not something you are going to be able to process quickly. You never gave close examination to how you would care for a baby. It was the goal. But now it is a fact.

Jim leaves for work. Your mother finally comes to collect you.

You immediately say to her, for reasons that you cannot quite understand, "Time to go visit Edie."

EDIE, WHO HAS BEEN suffering from cancer and is now in the final stages of that disease.

Edie Sees Her Husband

AFTER EDIE WAS ADMITTED to a nursing facility because her cancer was terminal, you and Jim used to visit her every Sunday, and Jim and Rory would play in the parking lot while you sat with your friend and chatted and laughed.

Now she has started to decline, and when you come out of the neurologist's office, it seems very important to go visit her right now.

In the car, your mother asks whether you would rather go home. She can tell you've been crying.

You say, "I really think we need to go visit Edie, because I just have this feeling that it is today that she's going to go."

Everything falls into place. Your mother arranges for someone to pick up Rory from school and you and she drive up to the nursing home.

Edie is in fact going to die today. It's obvious. When you walk into the room, she is flanked by her two daughters on either side of the bed.

A priest gives her the last rites. She is conscious and alert, and participates throughout the ritual. It's a surreal experience.

You are sitting next to her. She is very thin and her eyes are big, but she is totally coherent, and you can't stop looking at her.

Edie knew that you wanted to have another baby. She knew that you were hoping to again use all the bedding that she had made for Rory: the bumper pad, the rocking chair cushion, all the beautiful things that had made Rory's nursery so cheerful.

You say, "Edie, the doctor told me I can't have another baby."

She nods and says, "You shouldn't, honey. Think of Jim and think of Rory."

Think of Jim.

You say, "Well, I really wanted to use your bumper pads again."

"Well," she says, "save them for Rory when he has a child."

Here she is dying and you're sitting telling her about your little problem. But it's how you've always talked.

BESIDES EDIE THERE ARE FOUR OF YOU in the room: her two daughters, Mom, and you. She says good-bye to each person individually. People take turns sitting in the chair next to her to say good-bye. It's like Dorothy in *The Wizard of Oz* before she clicks her heels three times to go home.

IT'S YOUR TURN. She is holding your hand.

She tells you she can see her husband on a hill and he is waving to her to come to him.

She keeps saying, "Julia, how do I get there?"

It feels close and right for her to say your name.

"Julia, how do I get to him? How do I get there?"

"Edie," you say, "you have to do that on your own, and when you get there, what a nice welcoming it will be."

EDIE ALWAYS HAD the most beautiful silky white hair and gorgeous blue eyes, even at eighty-two. She was smart and she was beautiful.

As soon as her soul leaves her body, her body becomes a shell.

You stroke her hair, like you did on so many of your visits. Her once silky, snow-white hair appears to yellow instantly. It suddenly feels like hay. You notice her gaping mouth and see that her bright smile is gone and that her teeth seem to have darkened abruptly.

You think, "That's it, that's what it looks like. Her soul is gone and this is just a shell." Edie isn't in the room anymore. Only a shell.

DURING ONE OF YOUR LAST visits with her, you had asked Edie to send you a sign after death that she was okay. You told her that, if she felt like it, she could send you some money from the other side.

She always called you "honey."

Your father drives you back home. One of Edie's daughters has given you a little Winnie-the-Pooh bear to give to Rory. That bear is in the car with you and Dad. You bump it accidentally, and it says, "Have some honey, my friend."

You're startled. It's as if Pooh Bear had come to life.

It's Edie, so Edie. It's her saying good-bye. *"It's okay, honey. Think of Jim. Think of Rory. Honey, it's okay."*

And that's what she's saying now, somehow.

DEALING WITH THE FEELINGS of grief you have after Edie passes is a blessing.

The grief for her makes you put aside your issue about not having another baby. You can't allow yourself to be thrown into this depression. You have to deal with your emotions about Edie. And you have to think about Jim and Rory.

It's her gift to you.

"What Are You Going to Do After Your Stroke?"
"I'm Going to Disney World!"

PAUL AND GLENN SUGGEST taking a trip with them as a diversion for the whole family from the rigors of stroke recovery. Paul decides on Disney World. You think, why not, it's known for fairy tales—maybe you can make believe none of this ever happened. But you're apprehensive about going on the trip, what with the logistics and stress of traveling. Besides, being out of your element makes you uneasy. Paul reassures you. "Disney's perfect for you. They treat cripples great."

"You're only bringing me along to get a free pass to the head of the line," you say as a retort.

On the ride to the airport, you realize that you left your medicines on the kitchen table at home. You know you can't go without them, but you're afraid to own up. Finally, you do. Jim, agitated, turns the car around to retrieve the life-sustaining drugs. You think to yourself that this is going to be some trip.

Jim's completely silent.

This is his expression of anger. You want to scream, "Let it out! Let it out! Yell at me! Get it out so your blood pressure doesn't rise and then you have a stroke. Just yell at me."

From the backseat, squeezed between the luggage and Rory, Dad says he's never seen Jim so mad and notes that this silent treatment is much more effective than Mom's barking. Dear old Dad, ever the antagonist.

You arrive at the departure gate just as they are closing the hatch. This creates quite a stir for the passengers packed into the plane. As you hobble down the aisle to take your seat, you can feel all eyes on you. The scramble to make the plane exacerbates your stroke deficits. The left side of your face is sagging, and you're drooling. Your left arm is extremely spastic, flopping up and down as if attached to a puppet string. Your leg is stiff and hurts from being crammed under the seat in front of you.

By the time you arrive in Florida, you feel bent and twisted like a pretzel. The flight has taken more of a toll than you could have imagined. You stay positive though and look forward to better things to come in the land of magic. And the magic happens as soon as you arrive at the beautiful resort. Upon checking in, you are informed that your party has been upgraded to your favorite ride—the concierge floor—where food magically appears at breakfast, lunch, and dinner, with snacks and drinks in between. What luck, you think, as if your stroke has somehow led to this good fortune.

YOU THINK YOU'RE in pretty good shape for someone who has had a stroke. You had been doing a lot of walking around the neighborhood back home in anticipation of the trip, but you sense right away that you'll need a wheelchair to get around. Being out of your own environment and in a strange, albeit wonderful place puts a strain on you physically. You eye the wheelchair and balk at the thought of surrendering to it, but if you don't use it, your whole party will suffer. Every destination here requires a lot of walking and you know you're just not up to it. You set aside your pride and resign yourself to planting your ass in the chair with wheels.

As you approach the Star Wars ride there are warning signs posted at all points of entry about the risks to people with health issues. You have just become Disney's worst nightmare. You've arrived at the gate in a wheelchair, a leg brace, and a neck brace, with every intention of going on this ride. The nervous attendant takes one look at you and says, "Please, ma'am, we recommend that you don't go on this ride."

"Why? I'm going to defend the ship as well as anyone else."

"The ride bounces you around a lot, which might not be the best thing for you."

"I know, but it's a risk I'm willing to take to claim victory over the dark forces. I'm prepared for battle. As Yoda says, 'Don't try. Do.' And that's what I'm doing."

The attendant is licking his lips, and if his eyes get any wider, he'll lose his eyebrows completely. Apparently, it isn't part of his training to allow disabled, yet fully armored, patrons into his fleet. He excuses himself and returns momentarily with his supervisor. The supervisor reiterates that you should forgo this ride.

"I'm going on the ship—my family needs protection. Do you want me to sign a waiver that you are not responsible?"

"No, that won't be necessary, but we want you to understand that you may be at risk of injury."

"I'll take my chances. May the force be with you."

IN THE AFTERNOON you and Rory go to the pool for downtime, while Jim goes for a run.

Rory immediately heads to the long, serpentine pool slide. After a few runs on his own he begs you to do it, too. Although you're leery of trying it, you consent because you want to show him that you can do anything you set your mind to. You hobble across the boardwalk and climb what seems like an endless set of stairs. The lifeguard tells you to sit and you use his shoulders as a railing to get into a seated position. You're sliding. Swoosh, into the pool below, water shooting between your legs and up your nose. Still submerged and trying to right yourself, you are sent flying. Mayday, you've been hit broadside by a torpedo. An overly anxious kid didn't wait the requisite interval and came immediately behind you, slamming his feet into you as you were struggling to your feet. You hobble back to the pool area.

Poolside once again, you settle into a latticed lounge chair. You plop yourself down, knowing full well that you are stuck there until you're ready for the struggle to extract your weighted body from the lounger. You take note of Rory's gleeful squeals as he splashes in the pool.

When you're ready to get up, you anchor yourself with your left hand as you try to hoist your body up. Your hand slips through the chair webbing and smashes into the cement. You try again, now scraping your hand on the hard surface so that it bleeds. You are captive in the chair's web, like a bug in a spider's web.

Rory is standing by you, watching.

"Can I get the lifeguard to save you?" he asks.

"What? Their job is to save people from drowning in the pool, not to save people from drowning in lounge chairs."

This is war—you and the chair. You are going to conquer it. Using all your might, you somehow get yourself into an upright, if unsteady, position.

After a "relaxing" afternoon by the pool, you return to your room much the worse for wear from human torpedo strikes and web entanglements.

You say to yourself, "Did I really need to come all this way to go through a day like today?" Then you hear the excitement in Rory's voice as he talks about tomorrow's adventures, and the anticipation in Jim's voice as he enthuses about the restaurant you're going to tonight. Yes, you conclude, this really is worth it.

You're already thinking about the next adventure in the magical kingdom where dreams really do come true.

Out of the Blue

NOW THAT YOU ARE HOME, you have not only shoe envy, but pants envy.

You see women wearing these really cute Capri pants out there, but you have to stick with clothing that has elastic waistbands with no hardware. The truth is that you basically live in gym clothes during the week because of all the time you spend at the YMCA— but also because a lot of the activewear has elastic at the waist. You usually wear pants that have leggings so you can put your brace over them, but then you found "bootleg style" gym wear. It takes a while to get used to the brace being up against your skin.

You actually like having the pant leg over the brace. When the brace is visible, people stare at you and say, "What happened to your leg?" But when the brace is not visible and you're having a particularly spastic day and your stroke is being naughty, it looks like you have cerebral palsy. Then people don't ask anything.

A lot of times, if you're out shopping and you notice someone staring, you will say, "Do you want to know what happened to me?," and that will disarm them and give them the opportunity to learn that things really do happen out of the blue in this life.

Sometimes mothers hush kids and tell them not to stare. This feels wrong to you. You wish people would explain things to children; you wish parents would ask you, "Could you talk to my child about your injury?" You feel those are learning opportunities.

MARIE ONCE SAID to you, incredulously, "You act *happy* that you had a stroke—you treat it like a badge of honor."

You understand her point, but you know in your heart it's better to find some area in your life where you can grow than it is to find some area where you can complain. As for wearing your stroke on your sleeve, well, you can't exactly hide it, can you?

You refuse to believe there is any ceiling on improving yourself whether you have an injury or not.

And you want a pair of Capri pants.

Push Harder

YOU HAVE SIGNED UP to take part in a study of stroke survivors. The study is called a Personal Status Monitor.

The point is to give clinicians some sense of how well the patients are functioning at home. It's an area that needs investigating to see what can be done to improve at-home therapy and at-home awareness of what a patient needs.

So you have these electrodes on key muscle groups: on your legs, your back, your stomach, and your arms. You wear them for hours of repetitive activities. For instance, you have to pretend you're eating soup—it's really a bowl of water. You have to type on a typewriter. The interesting thing is, even though you think you're not using your left side with these exercises, the left-side muscles are showing up on the computer. It's interesting to see what is actually becoming involved when you don't think it is.

The hardest thing is to repeatedly pull your pants up and down. You have difficulty getting your pants around your waist with one hand; that really exhausts you. (You have shorts on, so you're not giving the researchers a glimpse of the moon or anything. You think it would be funny, though. You could have had something like "Surprise!" or "Moonstruck!" tattooed on your rear end.)

They tell you to button and unbutton a shirt. It's so frustrating; your real-life shirts are all sewn up these days: You can just put them on over your head. But the doctors keep telling you to button and unbutton the shirt. You're sweating like crazy and you can feel your carpal tunnel problems worsening, but it doesn't matter. They tell you to keep buttoning over and over again. You feel like slugging them. You feel like flipping them the bird with your left hand, but you can't do it yet. Anyway it would be rude.

Eventually, though, you realize that if you don't focus on the thing that's frustrating you, it's a little easier to do the exercise. Even if it's stupid.

The last item on the list of things you're supposed to do reads "bowel movement."

"Excuse me," you say, perusing the list, "but can we skip this one? Some things are meant to remain private."

It turns out they just want you to pretend, to use the muscles you would normally use *as if you were* having a bowel movement.

So there you are sitting in the chair, pretending to do a number two for them, but your muscles aren't showing up on the monitor.

"Is this exercise going to be studied by other doctors? I've always had a problem with constipation."

"Push harder," the guy behind the computer says.

So you push harder.

"Almost," he says. "I'm just barely getting it on the screen. Try pushing a little harder."

It's like you're in the delivery room, but you're trying to leave a different kind of deposit.

Eventually, you really go for it—a full-strength, grunting, groaning, 110 percent committed, no-plausible-deniability mock bowel movement.

And this is the moment your mother chooses to walk in the room to see if you're ready to be driven back home yet.

She stares at you there in the chair, then stares at the men at the computer monitors, then stares back at you.

"It's okay, Mom," you explain. "They're paying me a hundred bucks for this. Somehow, monitoring a bowel movement is going to help stroke patients. Anything for science."

YOUR HIPS RADIATE PAIN constantly because of the way you walk. Your gait has become so out of sync that your right hip, your unaffected side, will have to be replaced at some point. You also develop tendonitis in your right knee from the geeky walk. It flares up regularly and you have to ice it down.

Hemiparesis is similar to what Siamese twins have to deal with, where one twin is unable to use a leg or an arm. The other twin has to carry the load and do all the work.

You visit lots of therapists and take part in lots of studies. The pain arising from your gait problems will, you learn, be chronic, for the rest of your life.

The spasticity and pain do not let up, even with the various treatments you're undergoing. It's time to do something more long term: Botox shots. You've been told this will help with the spasms because the Botox will paralyze the antagonistic muscle and allow other muscles to work. Your physiatrist administers twelve painful shots a session in your leg, shoulder, and neck. As he places electrodes on your leg, the doctor explains that he has to electrocute the antagonistic muscle so that he hits the correct one. The shots only last three months.

"Hey, I have some crow's feet showing up on my face. Can you give me a little cosmetic treatment, too? Seriously though, speaking of feet—my foot is always in a clawlike position. Can you give my foot a shot, too?"

"Well, for me to relax the toes with Botox, you'd need to have the shot in the arch of your foot. There's no fat there, and it's extremely painful."

"I can't believe there's a body part on me that doesn't contain fat. Hell, it can't be that bad. Let's go for it."

■ ■ ■

THE DAY FOR YOUR PROCEDURE rolls around. Mom takes you to the doctor's office.

You know it's going to hurt like hell, and to brace yourself, you ask Mom to hold your hand. You've instinctively learned that holding another's hand during waves of pain helps alleviate some of it.

Your physiatrist has you lie on your stomach. You look back and get a glimpse of that needle. It must be eight inches long.

"Hey, I thought I was going to have a *needle* inserted, not a freaking sword! How many patients have you done this procedure on?"

"I've never completed one. People get squeamish when they see the size of the needle. You'll be my first. You sure you want to go through with this?" he asks.

IT DOES IN FACT hurt like hell.

But it works. Painted toes and sandals are now a possibility.

No pain, no gain.

Another System

One night, while watching the evening news, you see a report that certain cold medicines are being removed from the market because they contain a particular ingredient that can cause hemorrhagic stroke in young women.

You had taken a cold medicine the day you had your stroke.

You recall the name of the medicine and see it on the report's list.

Could this be what happened to you?

YOU SCHEDULED AN APPOINTMENT with your neurologist to discuss the cause of your stroke. The meeting was scheduled for September 11, 2001, at eight in the morning.

As you're driving to the appointment at 7:30 A.M., you tell Jim about this weird dream you had the night before. It was a restless night. You dreamed that your body was an airplane and you were flying people on your back across the country. You were flying them through hazy purple clouds.

You felt very sad.

Your meeting with Dr. Neuro is a fateful one. After reading

the latest research, he tells you that he is completely convinced that your hemorrhage was caused by the cold medicine you took prior to the onset of your hemorrhage. He says he's sorry that this information wasn't available at the time of your stroke.

But this is what caused the stroke.

"You are a classic case of the study for causation," he tells you. "Young, one-time dosage, and hemorrhagic stroke within hours. You're lucky you survived; most people don't make it after experiencing a hemorrhage such as the one you had."

If you had followed Dr. Jerk's treatment plan, you'd still be having chemotherapy every month to treat a disease you don't have, and your quality of life would be abysmal.

You are deeply grateful for the certainty. You thank Dr. Neuro for listening to you and caring for you as if you were a member of his family.

EXITING THE ELEVATOR in the main lobby after your appointment, you spot a television monitor on the wall, broadcasting the sickening image of a plane hitting the World Trade Center.

"HELLO, MRS. GARRISON, how are you feeling today?"

It's a quick, dutiful pleasantry. You can tell instantly that the judge—a tall fellow with piercing eyes and rimless spectacles—doesn't really care how you feel. But you figure you should answer anyway.

"I feel very spastic, but that's because I'm nervous. The five-hour ride here wasn't easy for me either."

"Do you feel well enough to answer a few questions?"

"Yes."

"When did you know that it was the medication you took that caused your stroke?"

"I didn't know for sure until September 11, 2001, when I met with my neurologist, after he reviewed the research. I'm certain of the date because everyone in America remembers that day."

"The defense believes that you knew it was the medication—or should have known—the first day you went to the hospital."

You're stunned. You can't comprehend what he's saying or what he's driving at. But you're supposed to say something.

"Huh?"

It's not a great response, but it's all you've got.

"How could I possibly have known about it the day I went to the hospital? I was having a stroke. The best doctors in the world didn't know at that point—the study hadn't even been released yet. Anyway, what difference would it make?"

"It makes a difference because the defense believes the statute of limitations is up. They say it's too late for you to prosecute."

You can feel yourself getting hot. You start to feel under attack.

The judge continues his pointed questions in a robotic fashion. He says he's concerned that you may not be able to endure a trial.

"If I can endure a massive hemorrhagic stroke," you say carefully, "I assure you I can endure a trial. The pharmaceutical company knew it was using something dangerous, but it was too cheap to change it. They need to be held accountable."

"Mrs. Garrison," he says matter-of-factly, "it has nothing to do with you or the merits of your case; it's based on the law. The statute of limitations period started ticking when you entered the hospital."

"Even though no doctor in the country knew that this cold medication was a problem at that time?"

"Yes," he says.

"Isn't that kind of a Christmas present for the pharmaceutical company?" He scowls at you.

Why are you being held accountable to a higher standard than the pharmaceutical company? They weren't required to remove the products from the market until the study was revealed—even though they suspected a problem and initiated the study.

■ ■ ■

A FEW DAYS LATER you receive formal notification that your suit against the pharmaceutical company that produced the medication will not go forward.

Your case has been dismissed without prejudice in the New Jersey court. Not because you didn't suffer injury as a result of this drug, but because the pharmaceutical company has unlimited funds to pay a vast number of lawyers who could knock you out on a technicality. Justice for sale.

One more complicated system you are no longer innocent enough to believe in.

You want this chapter of your quest for truth and justice behind you—but your brother John sees a chance to prevail. The New Jersey dismissal allowed a stipulation that you could refile your case in Massachusetts—where the statute of limitation laws are more lenient.

Massachusetts. Bring it on.

Promises

YOU DROPPED RORY off at school today without having to promise anything. A major victory.

RORY WAS SO YOUNG when your stroke occurred. He couldn't express his feelings until he could vocalize and verbalize. He was terrified, but he didn't have the ability to express how he felt.

So by seven and a half he had become extremely phobic, fearful of extraordinary things that don't happen to children, like, for instance, a heart attack or brain hemorrhage. Separations were a major challenge.

You would drop him off at school, and he would say, "Something bad will happen to me before I see you again. I know it."

You would drop him off to play with friends, and he would say, "Promise me nothing is going to hurt you today."

You would be getting him on to the school bus, and he would say, "Promise me Daddy won't get hit by a car today."

At first, you say, "Don't worry, nothing bad is going to happen, I promise."

But soon, you and Jim realize, he is relying on this promise of yours in order to start his day.

It's a big, fat lie. You know now that no one can predict what fate has in store for you.

It becomes very stressful for everyone. He's terrified that something violent or painful or life changing will happen to him, to you, or to Daddy every time you separate, whether it's going to bed, going to school, whatever.

One day, you're both in the car, and he asks you to promise that you won't die while he's away at school. You take a deep breath.

"Rory," you say calmly, "I can't promise you anything like that, because I don't know what's going to happen today."

It's the first time you've actually said it out loud to him—or, you realize, to yourself. You don't have control over the future, only your own choices. You don't know what's going to happen. None of us do.

"So," you continue, "I can't make that promise. Anything can happen. I wish I could change that for you, but I can't. Nobody can. But here's a promise I can make you. I promise that you'll have a great day if you have an open mind and a positive attitude. Your day will be much better if you do that than if you don't."

"MOM, I HATE BEING THIS WAY. I don't want to be scared all the time."

Rory says it flatly on the way to school. It breaks your heart; you know you need some help.

You decide to take him to your friend Janie's house—she has a lot of experience with children who've gone through trauma. But when the moment comes, Rory won't get out of the car. He cries and says he doesn't want you to leave him.

You walk him to the front door. He's still crying.

Janie, bubbly, answers the door and takes his hand.

"You know what we're going to do today, Rory?"

He shrugs.

"We're going to bake chocolate chip cookies together."

This distracts him enough for you to be able to slip away.

You return an hour later. Janie has made great progress. She has learned (while keeping him busy baking) that he doesn't want you or Jim to say good-bye or good night because he believes he won't see you again.

You agree to say *"See you later"* or *"See you in the morning"* instead.

AT EACH SEPARATION you've been walking him—and yourself— through the painful fact that you can't ever promise someone that nothing terrible will happen. Bad things *do* happen. It's how we react to them that determines our situation.

Today you dropped him off at a birthday party, and you heard him say, with your own ears, "Okay. The party's supposed to be over at four. See you then, Mom."

And you watch him hop out of the car and bounce up the stairs with his gold paper–wrapped present in his hand and a smile on his face.

partFIVE

A Stroke of Luck

MEMORIES ARE my most treasured possession. Memories can soothe you or they can cripple you. This book has been about memories.

Although I have had to summon the past, and shape it, for this book, I try not to remain in it; I work only in the present. And even though I know I have a long, possibly difficult journey ahead of me, trying to improve more each day, pursuing my legal case as well, I try not to live for the future, either. I believe each moment we experience really should be our most important moment. That's a hard standard to meet, but it's a bad one to ignore.

In hindsight, I've been able to review my choices, not always the best ones, but I've tried to take the lesson from the aftermath and grow. It is hard to believe that simply trying to relieve common cold symptoms would have changed my life forever. It proves that every choice one makes, no matter how benign it may appear, has a consequence. I have come to accept that things happen for reasons, and it is the Plan.

For every action, there is a reaction.

Since that first homage to my hemorrhage party, I have continued to celebrate the anniversary. Celebrating something absurd is a great decision, a way to take control of life. That's the key, not just living life passively but making decisions and choosing to grow.

People tell you, "Look at the glass as though it's half full, not half empty." Actually, I always want to look at the glass as half full—*and*. As in, the glass is half full, and where is the pitcher to fill the rest of it? I always want more, especially when I'm celebrating. It's important to never pass up an opportunity for the bubbly! I'm satisfied with the things that I have, but want to keep growing: spiritually, physically, in my family life, everything. Okay, not everything. When I say physically, I don't mean getting larger, I mean getting stronger. It reminds me of when I made my yearly visit to my grandparents in Pennsylvania. My grandmother would pick me up at the airport and squeal, "My, Julia, you've grown so big!"

I didn't accept it as a compliment. "Grandma, that's fine if you're talking to a toddler, but I'm twenty-two years old." She would make this same remark every year.

All my life, my glass has overflowed; it just happened to get knocked over when "the incident" occurred. Now, P.S., it's a matter of righting the glass and refilling it, but this time with a different and more meaningful substance.

MY STROKE WAS a devastating injury, one that didn't happen only to me, but also to my husband, my son, my parents, my siblings, and my friends. Yet in a way that is hard for an outsider to understand, my injury was also a great gift. I say that because I didn't recognize all the blessings I had before my stroke. I thought I did, but I know now that I didn't. Back then, I was only looking at the obvious blessings: home, family, and job. Now I know, as I never knew before, what a gift from God it is to sit up, to walk, to eat, to drive, to have family time, to be independent, and to share this life with someone who, you know with absolute certainty, truly loves you. The material things we give become obsolete, but to give of oneself—an act of kindness, for example—lasts a lifetime and beyond. To choose to share time with someone you love, knowing full well that your time on earth is limited, is a moment in time that is precious and will never come again.

These lessons are miracles, and I am grateful for them. In some ways (not, perhaps, in the ways I expected), I have to admit that my whole life after my injury turned into a miracle—however skeptical I may have been about such matters at various points in my recovery. I should not be here, but I am.

I once said to my dear Dr. Neuro, "I owe a lot to God for how far I've come."

He said, "Give yourself some credit, too. God could have told you to get out of the wheelchair, but you could have said no."

This may be true on the surface, but I know in my heart that it is equally true that God gave me the will, the spirit, and the sense of humor—and the optimism—to overcome this devastating injury. Now most people think I'm in recovery from a car accident. That might not *seem* like a victory, but consider that the right side of my brain consists mostly of dead tissue and contains a sizable hole. Yet the rest of my brain took over enough to allow me to function capably, if not perfectly, in an able-bodied world.

When I hear the words "stroke victim" I cringe. We're only victims if we choose to let ourselves be consumed by something. I'm a survivor who continues to thrive.

My real purpose in life—my new life, not the one I had before—started, unbeknownst to me, right after my stroke. Initially, when I was in the critical care hospital, people looked at me—paralyzed, fighting to live. I could see in their faces the sadness and fear of how things can happen to human beings without warning. Nurses, doctors, and visitors all commented on how young I was to be so injured. This sort of thing was only supposed to happen to older people.

Life was supposed to make sense.

Wings and Ladders

JIM AND I WERE DRIVING home late one night when we got a flat on the highway. We could hear the tire shredding. Jim had no choice but to pull over onto the shoulder. Not only was it a dangerous area, but it was pitch-black and pouring rain. With no flashlight, Jim struggled to locate the jack and tire iron buried in the trunk. It was pretty bleak, but then a nondescript delivery truck pulled over. A man got out and, without saying a word, went to work getting out the tools and changing the tire. He did this in complete darkness and there was not one word of conversation. Once he completed the task he ran back to the truck and drove off. I never saw his face and he didn't speak. We tried to give him money but he was gone. I didn't see any wings, but I honestly think he was an angel. I think he was setting an example for us.

Initially, my goal was to become who I was before the stroke. I was really in search of my full-functioning body. I remember shopping with my mother. I was in a wheelchair purchasing clothes for Rory. A young woman was in the same area of the store. As I stared at her (though she was oblivious of me), I thought, "I used to be just like her." At the time, it upset me that I was not like her. What I now realize is that I didn't even know her. I was looking at the outer appearance. This realization magnified the fact that I didn't really know me. But I have begun, I think, the process of knowing myself through the process of recovery. And yes, that entire process has been a gift from God.

I used to make deals with God. When I first found myself in a hospital bed, paralyzed, I asked God to let me feed myself and become independent. Once that was achieved, I prayed that I would be able to pick up my toddler and be able to put my arms around my husband again. As God answered my prayers, I continued to ask for more while expressing gratitude for what I had received. This has helped me come to terms with the fact that none of us ever really knows what is around the corner on our life's paths.

I thought my life path was to be a woman climbing the corporate ladder while maintaining a family life with a husband and two children. Instead, I got to climb a different ladder and learn that the ladder to God is a choice and that we can choose which rung we want to claim in our relationship with God. I thought I was a good person before this injury, but what I've learned is that I have to give something of myself in order to help others get through whatever may have them trapped.

When I awoke from surgery, I felt sure that I had a mission, a purpose in life. I wasn't sure if I'd ever get to know what it was. Now, I know that I have the privilege to be here, to share life with others, to find ways to give back to people who need something. I like to think that this book has been part of that mission, and that this story will help people overcome some of the all-too-easy "certainties" that they imagine define their lives.

"Young people aren't supposed to have strokes."

Aren't they?

"You have your whole life ahead of you."

Do I?

These are assumptions most people make in order to get through the day. I used to make them, too. Replacing them took a lot of work. To reach a point where you can really, honestly accept an event like a massive cerebral hemorrhage as part of God's plan requires not only your own willingness to take the next step on the ladder, but also, perhaps, the act of opening yourself to the possibility of receiving assistance from someone with wings.

Nowadays, my recovery lets me see the expression of relief on people's faces. It lets me see them acknowledge my progress, but also in that misleading "certainty" that bad things only happen to people who have lived for a long time—or to people who "deserve it." Or, the "certainty" that our mortality is a far-off reality, if it is a reality at all.

I try to correct them, but not like I would have corrected someone at work before my stroke. I try to tell them what I've learned: "Love your family, go home and kiss your spouse and kids. It's always best to have the warmth of love, even when you're apart from the person you love."

I don't know whether I'm going to wake up tomorrow morning. Nobody does. But I *know* I don't know that, and a lot of people imagine that they can be certain about tomorrow morning.

I truly feel like my stroke has made me a better person. It has given me the insight to see that there's more than meets the eye in any moment, any situation. My spirituality has evolved. I know I am here, for a while, in this body, because I made a choice and because God made a choice. While I'm here, I'm completely comfortable in my own skin. What a sense of freedom.

I believe that although I was a good person before the stroke, I was only tapping into a single facet of the diamond in the rough that we all are. Hopefully, by the time I complete my mission here on earth, I'll have become a multifaceted jewel. Every day I have a chance to add a new facet. I love diamonds.

I have angels around me all the time; they tell me things. For instance, there was a day when I was driving alone with Rory for the first time since my stroke. He was only three and I was nervous because my body was not in good shape. I was dragging my left side around. I decided that I was going to take him to a local park. On my way there—it is less than ten minutes from my house—I had a vision of Rory running, and in my vision he fell down. When he got up, there was blood all around his mouth and coming out of his nose.

It was a terrifying image. I panicked for a second and was about to turn around because of this vision, but instead I said a prayer to let me carry on; I needed to do this trip for my independence and to reclaim my role as a mother. I needed to do it for my son while keeping him from harm. I said a little prayer (it was more like a chat with God) and I continued on my way to the park.

The park has a couple of benches around the play area, which is one big sandbox that contains jungle gyms, tire swings, and forts and ladders. It is really a great place for kids. I had to sit at the bench farthest away. The other ones were full because there were many children playing. Two women came over and sat next to me on the bench. We talked a little bit. I had brought a book, but was too nervous to read, so I just watched my boy have fun; it made me smile.

I looked up and I saw him running as if he were in slow motion and he did a face plant right in the sand. My heart stopped. I froze as I witnessed the fall. The two women sitting beside me jumped up and ran over to him. I hobbled my way to where he sat crying. When he looked up, it was just like my vision. But instead of blood pouring out of his mouth and nose, it was only sand.

This type of vision and a knowing sense happens to me a lot. I get a little frightened by it because sometimes these visions come true. They do not make sense to me, and I do not know what they mean when it happens. I've learned not to make snap judgments of others, because the outer package is only good for a first impression. You need to go beyond the surface for a better understanding. I've discovered that I can no longer be embarrassed. There are many things that, before my stroke, I would have considered embarrassing. When I ask people what they think the word "embarrassment" means, the response is often "shame" or "humiliation." I now know it means judgment—others judging you. No one has the right to judge another. The only judgment I'm accepting is God's. So when you see me Rollerblading with my cane Steady and I happen to wipe out, you can laugh. I'll be laughing, too. Falling is just another way of moving forward.

BECAUSE I WAS RECOVERING during much of Rory's formative years, I was not able to teach him common tasks like tying a shoe, buttoning a shirt, or snapping his pants. But I have been able to teach him about people, and about being kind and about showing compassion. In fact, compassion has become a teaching platform for me to pass down to my son. I want him to realize that helping others is more rewarding than helping yourself. I want him to feel the power of positive thinking and attitude—the joy of seeing challenge and opportunity in adversity, which makes a victory more worthwhile.

When struggling for a title for this book, I looked to my young son and said, "Rory, help me come up with a title, I'm lost." Without missing a beat, he said, "How 'bout *My Curtains Were Closed and Now They're Open?*"

"What do you mean by that, Rory?"

"Well, before your stroke you couldn't see everything—and now you can. If you don't like that one, what about *God Showed Me the Way?*"

His insightfulness has shown me that I'm not the only one who has learned something on this journey.

Life took on an intensity after the stroke that I wasn't able to experience before. I learned firsthand that things happen for reasons, and sometimes we get to know why and sometimes we don't. But there is a Plan.

And I have come to accept that.

I know that no answers are possible outside of God, but I can't really tell you what I mean by that. I'm just thankful there is an answer, even if I don't understand it, and I lean on that answer, whether or not it makes sense to me at the time. A lot of people come out of an experience like this convinced that they have no control over their lives. I try to make things happen in the most positive way possible. Who has time to wait? God put us here to do something.

There really are angels, and if you listen, they're always looking for a way to guide your steps, always looking for a way to explain something to you. They're saying life is funny and difficult and pretty damn good, and when you can hear their message, even if it's just once in a while, even if it's very faint, you're deeply grateful—and you're never quite the same again.

P.S.: Thanks for all my blessings. I love life.

acknowledgments

Acknowledgments

Special thanks to . . .

Original Manuscript Editor: Brandon Toropov, Beachbrook Productions
For culling reams of material to get my vision of a good read.
Thanks for climbing the mountain with me.

Author Photo: James Fox
Like father, like daughter? They say we're so much alike, it's scary.
I inherited your humor. Thanks for the "funny" gene.

Mom Fox
For being my chauffeur, laundress, housekeeper, babysitter, closet
organizer, note taker, sounding board. Have I left anything out?
Yes, best friend. Bet you never thought you were going to have to
raise me twice.

My dear family and friends
For your support and encouragement, and for making me laugh even when I wanted to cry. Thanks for always being there for me.

Linda Wilkes, Northeast Visual Communications
For your breadth of knowledge and creative spark. You are a true Renaissance woman.

I had over forty physicians caring for me after the "incident." Two doctors who went above and beyond the call of duty I need to thank personally, and they are:

Kinan Hreib, M.D., Ph.D., Director of Stroke Services Neurology
For your medical expertise and for your insight and compassion. From the beginning, you listened and heard what the patient had to say. You are the best.
David Burke, M.D., M.A., Associate Professor, Harvard Medical School, Department of Physical Medicine and Rehabilitation
For the generous doses of laughter to offset the pain of those shots you give me. Your humor is as much a gift as your medical treatment.

Robert Drillio, IAM Orthotics
For keeping me on my feet and moving in the right direction.

Pam Hinckley and Carrie Myles
For keeping my body toned and supple. Hey, a girl can dream, can't she? For helping me get the most out of what I'm left with.

Dr. David Elpern and John St. Augustine
You are both kindred spirits who have taken up the drumbeat of the message. Thank you for your continuing support.

Chip Seelig, Mike Shatzkin, Vicky Bijur, and Marjorie Braman
The circle started with you, Chip, who believed in me and my work. You introduced me to Mike, who suggested I talk to Vicky, who presented my work to Marjorie, who believes in me and my work. The circle is complete, but the work continues.

I never really had a fire in my belly to write a book; it just seemed like so much work. All I ever wanted was to have one dedicated to me. Funny how life's journey doesn't always stay on course.

Julia Fox Garrison,
November 2005

appendixes

A Prescription for a
Productive Doctor's Visit

We come into this world seeing a doctor, and we continue to see a doctor until we reach the end of our journey. And while we're here, insurance companies dictate how long we get to spend with a doctor each time we see one.

Use this checklist to get the most out of your doctor's visit:

• Write down on an index card all medications, including prescription and over-the-counter drugs and diet supplements. Note the respective strengths and dosages. Keep the card accessible and up-to-date. Every doctor you see will ask for this information. You want to be accurate and consistent.

• Come prepared with a list of questions and concerns about your health in general and specifically about the condition for which you are seeking treatment.

• Have a family member or trusted friend accompany you into the examining room. You will have to filter a lot of information, so it helps to have an extra set of ears. Have the person take notes if possible.

• Ask about options for treatment, including alternative medicines, and possible side effects.

• Ask about additional resources that might be available to you, for example, Internet Web sites, studies, support groups.

• Have the doctor set your expectations as regards follow-up on what you have discussed today. When is the best time to call if you have additional questions? Will the doctor call you directly with test results? Is there an e-mail address that you can use for contact?

• Don't accept anything less than coequal status. Don't allow yourself to be talked down to or patronized. If you are dissatisfied or uneasy about your interactions, change doctors without a second thought.

• Go with your gut. If your body is telling you there's something wrong, trust your instinct—who knows your body better than you? Persist in finding the root cause; don't accept any suggestion that "it's in your head."

• Positive Outlook = Positive Outcome works. If you approach your consultation with a positive attitude and a sense of purpose, your doctor will respond in kind, and together you can work toward the desired result—a healthier you.

• Laughter is a great stress reliever and icebreaker. Use humor in your interactions to humanize the experience with your doctor.

An Open Letter to
All Doctors

Dear Doctor,

As your patient, I feel fortunate to be working with you and believe our partnership will provide the best possible outcome. Your knowledge and experience combined with my commitment and determination will make it happen. I look forward to our relationship.

Besides being a patient, I am a daughter, wife, and mother. Before I became a patient, I was a business professional. My makeup—family, childhood, education, work experience, relationships, values—defines me as unique. Because I am an individual, I do not fit some cookie-cutter mold that says I will respond in a certain way to my illness. Please treat me accordingly.

You may think that I am in denial over my illness. Understand that my mind hasn't yet grasped what has happened to my body. Let me ask the questions before you provide the answers. That way, I can come to understand what has happened to me and accept it on those terms. Then work with me to set goals that I can measure to see results.

I recognize that the insurance companies dictate how health care is dispensed and that is why your schedule is so tight, often causing you to fall behind. I'm all too familiar with waiting rooms. Those of us who are patients must by definition be patient. I do appreciate it, though, when you acknowledge the time I've spent waiting. While my time with you in consultation may be limited, remember that I and my loved ones must cope with my illness 24/7. With that in mind, you can greatly relieve my anxiety by setting my expectations with respect to follow-up and future contact, be it another appointment, phone call, e-mail, or something else. You might also consider providing a handout such as a list of frequently asked questions, Web sites, or reference materials that offer additional information about my condition. This would help to reduce my uncertainty and make our time together more productive.

Something else I would ask you always to be sensitive to—my dignity. Remember, above all else, I am a human being, not just a mass of protoplasm. Don't put a label on me because the classic symptoms of my illness predict a certain behavior when what you are witnessing may just be a part of my personality. If you have grim news, lead me to it gently but honestly, and always hold out hope. As my partner, I want you to share my motto: Positive outlook = positive outcome.

As a doctor, you are highly educated, but don't ignore that font of knowledge before you: me. I've spent a lifetime in this body; I know it intimately. Ask me what I think. And when you acknowledge that you don't have all the answers and that perhaps I should seek another opinion, I will only admire you more, for your humility. After all, we have a common goal—getting me well.

Thanks for hearing me out. I know I've put a lot on your plate, maybe more than your Hippocratic oath prepared you for. But when you accept me as your patient, you also take on the role of educator, adviser, and confidant. One more thing: Come equipped with a sense of humor. Sometimes it can be the best medicine.

With hope and gratitude,
Your Patient

Basic Dos and Don'ts
for Doctors

Lead. Lead the patients without using murky medical jargon.

Inspire. Inspire your patients to create their own goals.

See. See the unique characteristics of each patient.

Trust. Enable your patients to feel safe and confident.

Encourage. Provide positive words of hope, courage, and support.

Nurture. Treat the mind as well as the body.

Don't try to be God.
Do recognize that you have a gift from God.

Don't treat your patient as a number.
Do acknowledge that every patient is unique.

Don't assume that drugs are always the cure.
Do promote healthy alternatives—diet, exercise, overall well-being.

Don't treat the symptoms only.
Do treat the root cause.

Don't limit the parameters of the treatment.
Do think outside the box—acupuncture, natural, meditative.

Don't introduce negative patient labels.
Do provide positive feedback and encouragement.

Don't be too busy to return calls.
Do set expectations on when and how you will get back to your patient.

Don't ignore a patient's intuition.
Do put your trust in the relationship.

Don't put limits on the outcome of recovery.
Do suggest that improvement is ALWAYS possible.

Don't assume that you are the superior in the relationship.
Do accept that you are an equal partner.